2023 LONGHORN FOOTBALL PROSPECTUS

11TH ANNUAL
THINKING TEXAS FOOTBALL

AUTHOR: PAUL WADLINGTON
PHOTOGRAPHER: WILL GALLAGHER

Contents

Greetings!

Welcome to the 11th annual 2023 Longhorn Football Prospectus: Thinking Texas Football. The Burnt Orange Bible is a Texas football preview, a season companion and reference guide, and a resource for the entire 2023 football season.

Thinking Texas Football, in deference to its name, is written for an intelligent football layperson. It won't insult you by writing down to the lowest common denominator nor will it try to overawe you with technical babble. The book's best ambition is to provide you with different tools – while plainly communicating an awareness of its own biases and blind spots – so that we can engage in a conversation that mutually enriches our shared passion.

If you want to see this preview continue to be published and support independent media, please write a 5 star review and share it with your tribe in real life and on social media. Word of mouth is our lifeblood and the only way to guarantee future editions. This book can't continue without your support!

Hook 'em!

Hello SEC, Good Riddance Big 12

What better way to start a 2023 Texas and Big 12 football preview than looking forward to the 2024 Southeastern Conference?

Probably not the best marketing strategy for this book, but the massive elephant in the room needs to be acknowledged before asking him politely to return in a year after we've built a proper enclosure and counterfeited a therapy animal certificate so we can bring the big guy on airplanes.

Checking any bags today? No, just this trunk.

The Texas Longhorns are headed to the SEC.

If you can't beat 'em, join 'em! That might sound like a defeatist refrain, but Texas and Oklahoma's 2024 move to the Southeastern Conference is one of the most meaningful realignment moves in college football history and, far from defeatism, it is cause for celebration. The other primary celebrant? Television networks starved for more live content that they can sell ads against to an affluent demographic in an antiquated 70 year old revenue model kept alive only by the passions of live sports fans.

The move is not motivated by resignation but calculation and optimism. At their athletic best, both Texas and Oklahoma have proven that they can compete with any team from any conference. In down years, Texas can still print money like the Federal Reserve after a Vegas weekend bender. So why go at all? Why now? The simplest answer is that Texas finally has competent, bold leadership who understand simple market realities. Simultaneously, they capitalized on Longhorn fan disaffection for an increasingly undermining, resentful Big 12. The market forces are primary, but hard feelings were the necessary catalyst that made a move to the SEC doable, an idea that one decade ago was a cultural non-starter. Texas fans and administration finally found a backbone, got tired of being bitched at by the freeloaders, snapped out of their aimless lethargy, started worrying more about Texas

than dumb national media articles, and made a couple of phone calls. The SEC was delighted (well, not everyone, Texas A&M was displeased to find out that their understanding of Texas joining and the rest of the conference's understanding were very different) and ESPN did a backflip in ecstatic joy. As for the Sooners? "Finally! We were already packed. What took you so long? Uh, who is paying our buyout?"

Texas and Oklahoma will have to pay off the league on their way out the door (effectively, via transferred television rights payoffs for valuable non-conference games like Michigan in 2024) and ESPN and ABC overpaid the Big 12's new television rights deal as a sweetener to prevent the league from fouling an early Texas exit. The Big 12 securing a 2 billion dollar media deal through 2031 sounds like a big win for the league until one considers that the Big 10 re-upped for 7 billion on similar timelines.

The networks viewed lubricating the deal from the perspective of their larger book of business and whatever they lose or break even on with the Big 12 will be made up for and then some by the SEC and Big 10. When the Big 12 comes up again for renegotiation in eight years without leverage, unable to deliver appointment viewing or demography, reality will set in for a league that has been living under a Longhorn umbrella. For the first time, the Big 12 schools will experience a reckoning with their true market value minus Texas television sets. Only Madonna's bathroom mirror knows comparably terrifying truths. A league convinced of their market buoyancy will jump in the deep end without their Longhorn floaties. A pity that the lifeguards on duty will be watching Texas take on Georgia.

Why is it that Oklahoma – a school with a chip on its shoulder the size of Stonehenge – is able to cooperate with Texas? What explains the businesslike collaboration between two rivals in coordinating their exit partnership?

Adam Smith would be proud to see such pure economic self-interest spawning mutual cooperation absent affection, but the Longhorn-Sooner frenemy relationship is an interesting one, worthy of long hours of therapy to unravel, right after throwing a cup of beer at that fat guy in overalls doing a Horns Down. Oh, he was our therapy partner. Sorry. Bad start to the process. Let's reset.

It goes deeper than pure commerce. Unless you're referring to the Texas-OU fan brawls that used to mar Commerce Street in Dallas on the eve of the Red River Shootout. For both schools there is a vague comprehension that their destinies are intertwined, an eternal Joker to the other's Batman. Just like the vigilante and archvillain, mutual hatred creates purpose and mission. In the infamous The Dark Knight interrogation scene where Batman dismisses The Joker as a psychopath who wants to kill him, the Joker responds,"Kill you!? I don't wanna kill you! *What would I do without you*?"

Who dares end a rivalry where trading annual humiliations fosters such depth and clarity of purpose?

Contrast this to Longhorn fan attitudes when Texas A&M went to the SEC. The prevailing sentiment was "Don't let the door hit you on the way out" and "Eternal scoreboard" or "Now everyone else gets to experience how truly weird you are." Tell the average Texas fan that we will never play Oklahoma again and they will regard you strangely, furrow a brow, and say,"Even if splitting with them might hurt OU and have a negligible impact on us, we are compelled to play them."

Of course, Texas leaving was a decade too late in coming. In 2010, Texas flirted with the Pac 12 and the Big 10 while Sooner fans wondered if they wanted to trade in their big fish in small pond status that had been serving them so well. Mind you, they were going to go with Texas, no matter the destination. Like a wife whose husband tells her he wants to go to Thailand alone to "think about some stuff", Oklahoma would assert the privileges of married rivalry. Not without me, mister.

Oklahoma – whatever their recent run of gridiron success on the field over the Longhorns – understands that they are the junior partner in the Texas-Oklahoma hate symbiosis. Held prisoner by their fanbase's psychic need to torment Texas, by the reality of their own modest television markets and a program imperative to access Lone Star state recruiting. Throw in that the average Okie's life ambition is to beat Texas, own a waverunner and have a living room decorated with payment plan furniture under plastic and there you have it.

Even if Texas fans had mental blocks about the SEC as an option, the inevitability of that conference grew with each passing year. The Pac 12 proved flaky, unreliable and more interested in riding social currents than making adult reality-based decisions while the Big 10 checked a close second to the SEC in nearly every box. A fine alternative, but if you're going to be a bear, why not be a grizzly? The ACC was proposed by people who don't understand geography or that the league is the Big 12 redux on the verge of collapse; the money-making programs resent the freeloaders while the freeloaders resent their charity.

To make the SEC work, the Texas fanbase also had to get over a few things.

Like academics! Listening to Texas fans fret over SEC academics while sharing a league with Oklahoma State, Kansas State and Texas Tech for 25 years is...remarkable. But it was in the zeitgeist. The truth is that several of the major schools in the SEC have made real academic strides, reflective of the shifting demography of the country. On balance, they were already ahead of the non-Longhorn Big 12 and that gap will only grow. Texas made the same academic leap decades ago, elevated by the same demographic trends that the key states of SEC country are now experiencing in earnest. Truthfully, the most recent admissions policies in Austin have been degrading the academic brand, while schools like Florida, Georgia, Tennessee and Auburn are on the rise and Vanderbilt remains a Cornbread Ivy. The average Arkansas fan not knowing their times tables didn't affect Texas in the SWC and it won't affect us now. Also, why do you care so much, nerds?

Culture? Longhorns have always prided themselves on a certain cosmopolitanism, a contrast to their parochial neighbors. This attitude - sometimes legitimate, sometimes class snobbery – doesn't hold up much any more. Nashville, Atlanta and Palm Beach aren't exactly backwaters. Alright, alright. The road trip to Starkville will be anthropological in nature, but beyond that, get over yourselves. It's not like Baylor fans are a blast to hang out with. Give me Boudreaux the LSU fan forcing us to do shots and try his gumbo six hours before the game over Baylor fan Chazz Dockerslacks trying to find out if your Daddy is someone important in Highland Park and yearning for dancing to be abolished on campus again. Embrace the madness. It just means more.

Doesn't the SEC cheat? The moral argument! Clutch your pearls and retire immediately to the fainting couch. Of course they do! They want to win games. Buying athletes is a great way to do that. Every conference that Texas has ever been a part of cheated rampantly, brazenly and stupidly. The old Southwest conference was destroyed by overwhelming cheating and it earned SMU the death penalty. Texas A&M bought Eric Dickerson a maroon Trans-Am. That he drove to SMU. I didn't say there were always proficient cheaters. Oklahoma cheats and has always been a mercenary operation fueled by a not unsizeable number of sociopaths. One of the most amazing features of Sooner success is their ability to keep their sociopaths focused on football while quietly cleaning up their inconvenient off-the-field messes, only occasionally making the cover of Sports Illustrated with players in handcuffs. Baylor commits scandals so frequently at such levels of depravity that college sports fans use their school name as a verb. "You really Baylored that." Kansas basketball has more slush funds than a Baltimore politician. Shall we go on? Are we seriously taking a moral position based on the company we've kept?

In the new world of NIL, player portals and professionalized college sports, what exactly is cheating anyway? Schools entice college athletes in the open now. Including Texas. By the way, Burnt Orange patriots, go input your Platinum Amex digits into the Texas One Fund right now, right after buying ten more Thinking Texas Football previews and sending them to your friends. Bottom line: NIL has defanged cheating objections, weak as they were. No one wears a white hat anymore. Texas strives for light gray. There's no conference for Boy Scouts.

But, the SEC is really hard! Texas would do better playing in the Sun Belt. Ah, the competitive cowardice disguised as a tactical sophistication argument. Some Texas fans present statistical arguments as to why the Big 12 is the best path for a national title and that being a big fish (an underachieving big fish, mind you) in an increasingly irrelevant pond is preferable to playing primetime big boy football that might force uncomfortable growth. So, how has that worked out for us over the last decade plus? We've been killing it, right? This analysis ignores the fact that Texas must still be very good at football for the easy path conference argument to work. However, to be really good at football, Texas must be challenged. See the inherent contradiction? There is strong evidence that the University of Texas default state is an orgy of bureaucratic lethargy and make-work projects that pay out whether Texas goes 5-7 or 13-1. Bellmont expenses always rise in exact synchronicity with Longhorn revenues every year. No economies of scale ever realized. Remarkable, isn't it? If Texas can't create internal tension to force growth, we'd better find outside agitants.

The simple truth is that when Texas is challenged, it prospers. Or it is forced to clean the house and find winners. When Texas goes unchallenged and rendered complacent, it's a mess of underachievement and docility. The tactical weak conference argument is tantamount to contending that standout football players should stay in high school for additional years so that they can dominate feeble competition and give themselves the best path to the NFL. Of course, it doesn't work that way. That player would actually degrade while never being forced to evolve. Real competitors interested in progress understand they must test themselves against the best. Competition forces a reckoning and a leveling. Discomfort and the fear of humiliation spurs innovation and hard work. Joining the SEC is a dueling glove across the cheek. Is it gonna be Texas Fight or Texas flight? You are a Thinking Texas Football reader, thus you are attractive, smart and brave. Texas Fight is the only option for you.

As with NIL and cheating, a change in playoff structure also renders ideal conference path objections moot. A 12 team playoff means that a 9-3 SEC team with the third hardest schedule in the nation and close losses to Bama, LSU and Texas will be regarded as playoff worthy. They are also better prepared for playoff football than a 12-1 Conference USA champion with a schedule strength in the 80s. That does raise a related point: college football fans and analysts will learn to accept that 1-3 losses, once fatal to any college team's title ambitions, is now the price of doing business in the SEC and Big 10. NFL fans already understand that a 14-3 record in a league of competitive parity is excellent. College football super conferences will force college fans to embrace a similar mentality. Will we one day have a two or three loss playoff era national champion? Indeed we will. Count on it.

We know what was in this move for Texas. What's in it for the SEC? By adding Texas and OU, the SEC is now the league of the recent past, the present and the foreseeable future.

The newly constructed 2024 SEC has won 16 of the last 22 national championships (Texas 2005, Oklahoma 2000 add to the bounty) and the losing team in the other six games was usually a SEC school. Besides on field domination, the league will further control college football mindshare nationally – strengthening the perception amongst recruits that the games in other conferences are just appetizers to the real football played in the only league that matters. That's a bold assertion, made even more irritating by the fact that it will largely be true. If you thought SEC hype was unbearable before, you ain't seen nothing yet. It will certainly feel different sitting on the other side of it. The other conferences won't appreciate being treated as the G League or WNBA to the NBA and objectively, they have a point. But good luck persuading the best concentration of talent in the country – much of it distributed almost exactly on the SEC footprint – that they should bypass SEC campuses and network television domination to play their ball somewhere else. We're told that perception informs reality. This is often true. You know what really informs reality? *Perceptual reality built on actual reality.*

The SEC has always had fervor. Depth. Now it has span. Breadth. While the Big 10 can boast the most living alumni of any conference and can theoretically capture robust media markets like Los Angeles, Chicago, New York City, Boston or Washington DC, the reality is that the intensity of capture in Atlanta, Dallas, Houston, Austin and Nashville dwarfs the theoretical capture of markets that lack college football fan passion and college football fans everywhere want to watch good ball. More people in New York City will tune in to watch Texas and LSU than Rutgers and Boston College. A college campus being near a city does not capture the audience. Compelling football does.

The state of Texas is the great prize. The second most populous state in the country marries fervent fandom to massive demography and all future projections show these trends accelerating. Florida recently surpassed New York for the 3rd biggest state while Georgia is now ranked 8th with a bullet. Every populational trend line for Texas, Florida, Georgia, Tennessee, Missouri and South Carolina is rocketing up and to the left while Northeastern states, California and most Midwestern states bleed population or barely hold ground.

Texas A&M was the first vital inroad to the state's viewership and recruiting grounds, but the Longhorns are the prize that commits the state completely. TCU or SMU does not deliver DFW markets and UH doesn't deliver the city of Houston, much less Humble or Katy. Despite what their alumni and an alarming number of sportswriters believe. The state is owned by Texas and Texas A&M, in that order. In fact, of the major metro areas in Texas, only Lubbock – the 11th largest state population center – will be controlled by a 2024 Big 12 school. That's around 330,000 viewers in a state of 29 million. Even that hold may be tenuous when Texas Tech faces Cincinnati on the same day that Texas plays Oklahoma or Texas A&M plays LSU. Oklahoma can't deliver television sets in quite the same way as the Horns or Aggies, but a storied national program dedicated to creating a university that the football team can be proud of is no small asset for any athletic conference.

The wise decision to scrap internal divisions means that the SEC now has appointment programming every week. What was once considered epic viewing like Texas-Georgia, Alabama-Florida and Oklahoma-LSU will soon be normal weekly SEC programming. As for maximizing games of lesser national interest – say, when Mississippi State battles Kentucky or Texas takes on Vandy – there's the SEC Network. Don't confuse that impressive cash cow with the Longhorn Network and its relentless cuh-see-ta commercials. The SEC Network has a 4.8 billion dollar valuation without Texas and Oklahoma. What happens when they are added to the mix? A la carte cable packaging also means that any SEC or college football enthusiast will buy the package, whether they live in Boston or Mobile.

The SEC network is an impressive earner, favored by advertisers who are increasingly unimpressed with regular network programming as a vehicle for selling. . . well, vehicles.

This move, along with USC and UCLA moving to the other clear monster conference – the Big 10 – creates even more separation at the club between the folks who get face checked standing in line for three hours and those who are ushered in behind the velvet ropes. Whether that's good for college football or simply speeds the inevitable formation of elite mega conferences and ensures the demotion of several current FBS schools to de facto relegation is a moot point. It simply is. It's all being driven inexorably by market forces and practicalities as impartial as gravity.

Only one thing might have hindered these unfeeling forces: the human element. Specifically, deep sentimental relationships, the inertia of tradition, mutual respect and a shared conference culture.

The Big 12 had none of those things.

The truth is that the Big 12 was a mercenary necessity established in 1994, born of the hasty union between a population starved Big Eight and the once mighty but enfeebled SWC. The rivalries were genuine but a shared culture never cohered. Realignment was spawned by universities realizing that their conference affiliation was not a dusty landscape painting hanging in a museum never to be touched, but an etch-a-sketch that could be shaken and reoriented, with a more favorable picture drawn in its place. Don't like that one? Shake it up again. Once schisms begin in any institution built on tradition, adherence and obedience, they don't stop. They accelerate. Forget conferences, ask Martin Luther. He didn't anticipate his reforms leading to 33,000 new sub-denominations of Christianity. He didn't even think he was creating Protestantism. But when you open the door...

Attractive schools begin to date around and lose all sentiment for their first love. Unattractive schools were reminded painfully that loyalty is defined mainly by your options. Realignment shook the Big 12 deeply. Somehow from this vast universe of market forces, incurious and vacuous media blamed Texas for realignment despite the fact the entire economic structure of the Big 12 and its viability relied largely on the Horns. The Big 12 worked economically because of Texas and the Big 12 continued to live on because Texas stayed. However, when the facts don't agree with the assertion, yell the assertion louder.

Texas had the ability to effectively dissolve the league by leaving for the Pac 12 or Big 10 in 2010, consigning TCU and Iowa State to finding out their true individual values in the market (spoiler alert: they were low), but visionless Texas leadership consented to a massive network buy off with an inflated television contract spread equally across the entire Big 12 with the Longhorn-specific sweetener of the Longhorn Network. The LHN was an ESPN bribe not to upend the apple cart and a small test run for the more ambitious SEC Network. By remaining in the Big 12, Texas was the tide that every league boat rose on, but league mates still resented the Longhorns owning a yacht. If jealousy is obsessively wanting what another has, envy is not caring if your lot is improved just so long as what another has is destroyed. Those twin impulses drove the psychology of the Big 12 post realignment.

Texas delivered the league's television sets and financial viability while state of Texas recruits created lifelines for once moribund programs. Every other team in the league was a beneficiary, awarded Texas market driven contract money that they could have never commanded on their own. The result was that the other teams in the league exhibited gratitude and appreciation for their benefactor, while working cheerfully together to build a strong culture of cooperation and bonhomie. Just kidding. Instead, they blamed Texas for *being greedy for remaining and not disbanding the league* while Texas-fueled cash underwrote their programs. Amazing. Texas doesn't require thanks or anything less than a conference competitor's best effort on the field but the constant backbiting got old. Given a choice between becoming collaborative symbiotes or useless parasites, too many schools in the league chose to attack the host. Texas carried parasites because Texas leadership was too frightened or lacking in vision to burn them off, fearful that someone with a newspaper column might call them mean.

Amusingly, when BYU was first proposed as a possible league expansion option a few years ago, Texas was open to the idea of a potentially useful addition. It was the Big 12's least profitable and most insecure programs that objected. Their reason? Not wanting to split revenue. Oh, the irony.

This is a reminder that the two words most rarely heard at a public assistance office are thank you. If resentment is drinking poison while hoping someone else will die, then the rest of the Big 12 was in perpetual hemlock happy hour. The Longhorns slogged along in weird co-dependence, legitimately puzzled as to why the Horns could effectively underwrite the league yet play conference road games where the opponent didn't commit a single penalty and Texas had 14. The question isn't why Texas left the Big 12. The real question is: What took so long?

Texas didn't leave the Big 12 because of the distorted self-image of the other league members or their inability to grasp lemonade stand level economics. Market forces and a neighborhood upgrade were the drivers of the Longhorns saying vaya con dios, but the inability of Big 12 league mates to build a viable shared culture or understand the actual infrastructure supporting their sweetheart television deals, intertwined with the perpetual incuriosity of media drumming idiotic narratives made the departure all the easier. Pile up enough of it and the once unpalatable notion of joining the SEC became not only increasingly appealing, but inevitable.

If Texas fans glance back in the rearview as their U-Haul rounds the corner out of the old neighborhood, it's likely not from sentiment. More likely it's the hope that they might catch a faint glimpse of a distant streaking meteor blazing inevitably towards the center of the neighborhood that they paid for and that their free rent neighbors never stopped whining about. The driver's reflection off of that rearview won't be a frown. That's a smile.

Good riddance.

Can Texas Win The League?

Texas should be the clear favorite to win the Big 12. Caveats about injuries, disclaimers about sports being unpredictable and all other excuses are hereby acknowledged.

2023 Texas brings back 15 starters, signed an epic recruiting class and worked the portal like a Ritz Carlton doorman. No Big 12 team has more answers at more positions, exhibits better roster depth, has more high upside players at key positions, or returns more meaningful production on both sides of the ball. When you adjust for schedule, opponent and season long performance, the 2022 Longhorns were the 6th best team in the country by FEI (advanced metrics), a mere 25 points away from going undefeated. Given that Texas went 8-5, they were uniquely unlucky or had a knack for losing tight games. Perhaps both. If you blinded the teams in the Big 12 and simply offered their 2023 resumes, Texas is the choice. But predictions for Texas winning the Big 12 carry a lot of mental baggage.

What about underachievement? Or the other times that Texas Was Back, but was not back? Or that close loss in the Alamo Bowl? Didn't Quinn Ewers look shaky last year? Texas hasn't won the Big 12 since 2009. Superstar running back Bijan Robinson is gone. The defense didn't understand situational football in some key moments. How the hell did we lose to Texas Tech and Oklahoma State? Steve Sarkisian has never won ten games as a head coach. Texas was 2-5 in one score games. What if the Big 12's parting gift to the Horns is a series of Saturday snow jobs, courtesy of the zebras and the league office?

Those are the objections. Some emotional, some reasonable, some a little of both.

The hardest thing for any analyst to do is to begin each season anew and dispassionately assess the landscape. Narratives are not analysis. Some trends and history are relevant, others are a meaningless distraction. "I can't predict Texas' success until I see it happen!" Good insight. Most of us can also see something after it happens. Thank you for filling time and space with words.

Steve Sarkisian is only one game over .500 as the head coach at Texas. Over those two years, Texas is 4-10 in games decided by one score or less. That statistic can serve any master. It could be definitive proof of bad coaching and poor gameday management at key moments. Good coaches win close games, don't they? Or is it proof of a mediocre roster more interested in Friday nights on 6th street than Saturdays in DKR? Or is losing close games simply evidence of the thin margins between winning and losing for an inexperienced football team under new management? Losing 20-19 to Alabama in a hard fought game where Texas was on the wrong end of some bad calls goes down as a binary loss in the season record. On the other hand, losing to an Oklahoma State team in Stillwater that would go on to lose 5 of its next 6 doesn't suggest that Texas coached or played anywhere near its potential that day.

There's still another option: Texas has had major deficiencies in key areas that minimize the ability to win close games. At the risk of oversimplification, experienced offenses can make adjustments in-game, particularly if they have the right components at quarterback and on the offensive line. At the further risk of oversimplification, the right Jimmys and the Joes on defense running quality schemes stop opponent offenses on 3rd and 4th down. Game results follow.

In 2022, starter Quinn Ewers was a novice college starter who hadn't played a full year of football since his sophomore season at Southlake Carroll. He got hurt playing behind an offensive line starting two true freshmen and a true sophomore and threw to a number one receiver with a broken hand. That might lead to some disjointed efforts. Might solving the close game puzzle be as simple as getting more talented experience on offense and more overall talent on defense so that Pete Kwiatkowski can stop those back-breaking 3rd and 4th down conversions in tight games? It's as valid a premise as any. Perceptions of Sark's 3rd year at Texas are as influenced by disposition as by pure reason.

Meta-narratives are interesting and occasionally fun to pursue, but most of them are constructed retrospectively or deal heavily with correlations that may not have much causality behind them. Texas has the best squad in the conference given the facts we know at this time. What we know can shift though, can't it?

Sonny Dykes knew in September of 2022 that Chandler Morris was his best quarterback. Morris' injury and later benching allowed Big 12 Offensive Player of the Year Max Duggan to lead his team to a national title game appearance. The same benched quarterback that led TCU to a 3-6 conference record in 2021.

Chris Klieman believed in September of 2022 that Nebraska transfer quarterback Adrian Martinez gave his team the best chance to win. Will Howard was a known quantity who had in two years of prior action thrown more interceptions than touchdowns (9 to 11) and had a career passer rating that bore ribbons of shame. Naturally, Will Howard's ascendance to starting quarterback allowed the Kansas State Wildcats to win the Big 12 title as he threw 15 touchdowns and only 4 interceptions over the back half of the season.

The two teams that played for the Big 12 title in Dallas were led by quarterbacks who started the season as backups. Even head coaches can't always properly project their best players. And they watch them practice every day. It's like their job! How on earth are we supposed to predict anything?

Man predicts, God laughs. Most narratives are for dummies trying to make sense of an uncertain world. This preview doesn't really do narratives, but it will assess the landscape and help give you the tools to make your own predictions. The unexpected is likely. That doesn't mean you throw up your hands and say,"It's all a crapshoot! Why bother?" Like sports, the game of craps has percentages and probabilities. Playing the number 8 has substantially better odds than the shooter throwing double 6's. Bet accordingly.

In 2023, taking the Texas Longhorns is placing your chips on 6, 7 and 8. No one can control the roll of the dice, last season's rolls are irrelevant and the best team wins.

Unless it doesn't.

Modern College Offense: The Truth About Scoring

Who had the Big 12's best offense in 2022? And what exactly constitutes offense? Is it just points on the board? Or does a chosen offensive pace have implications for every aspect of your team? If you want to understand how to contextualize offense in the modern era, read on.

Last year, the Baylor Bears dropped 69 points on the Albany Great Danes while rolling up nearly 600 yards of offense, but it's meaningless whether they scored 49 or 69. The extra 20 points is padding, like a college freshman who discovers their dorm's meal plan. That padding lives on in their season statistics and smooths over the same offensive unit putting up only 3 points against Kansas State. Average them together and we're looking at 36 points per game of offense. Great success! Given that, let's reduce the statistical universe to conference play only.

Offense

The correlation between points per game and conference success can't be denied. Offense wins championships! Except that scoring is a **team measure**. The idea that offense is solely responsible for scoring ignores the contributions of defense and special teams to the final numbers on the scoreboard.

The 2009 Texas Longhorn team that played Alabama for the national title scored non-offensive touchdowns by the bushel on defense and set up the offense with countless short fields by forcing 37 turnovers (25 interceptions) along with safeties, pick sixes and lots of defensive mischief. Additionally, Jordan Shipley, Marquise Goodwin and DJ Monroe fueled a special teams group that scored an amazing seven touchdowns on kick returns and punt blocks. 2009 Texas scored a lot of points, but closer examination reveals that the offense was a more modest component of scoring than one might imagine.

Rank	Team	Games	TD	FG	XPT	2XP	PTS	Avg/Game
1	TCU	10	49	15	44	1	385	38.5
2	Texas	9	40	12	40	0	316	35.1
3	Kansas State	10	43	15	43	0	348	34.8
4	Texas Tech	9	35	16	31	2	293	32.6
5	Baylor	9	35	8	32	2	272	30.2
6	Kansas	9	37	5	34	0	271	30.1
7	Oklahoma	9	34	9	33	1	268	29.8
8	West Virginia	9	31	8	24	0	238	26.4
9	Oklahoma State	9	24	19	21	0	226	25.1
10	Iowa State	9	17	9	16	0	147	16.3

TCU was the best team scoring team in the conference last year, but their defense and special teams chipped in nicely. That's how they won 7 conference contests by 10 points or less and earned a playoff spot. Note that the top 3 teams in scoring offense were the ones in the hunt late with two represented in the conference title game. Points on the board are a good thing, but it's important to understand that points get on the board by means other than offense.

Do the Oklahoma State numbers shock anyone? Bad OL play and an erratic, oft injured Spencer Sanders contributed heavily to that feeble metric. Iowa State couldn't advance the ball and couldn't get it in the end zone when they did. The Incel Offense. Let's dig in a little deeper, control better for team scoring, and look at pure offensive efficacy...

Offensive Yardage/Per Play

Yardage can be empty calories if you don't control for pace. The easiest way to control for pace is to look at yards per play. When you do that, the truly dangerous offenses come to the fore and paper tigers are lit ablaze.

Texas Tech team scoring, aggression on 4th down and frenetic pace gave the illusion of competent offense. Yards per play and functional eyeballs tell us differently. Oklahoma State also used pace to partially obscure that their offense was about as effective as Iowa State's on a per play basis.

Rank	Team	Games	Rush	Pass	Plays	Yards	Av/Play	TD	AV/Game
1	Oklahoma	9	1899	2265	695	4164	6.0	34	462.7
2	TCU	10	1954	2665	710	4619	6.5	46	461.9
3	Texas Tech	9	1525	2563	769	4088	5.3	35	454.2
4	Kansas State	10	2007	2391	684	4398	6.4	42	439.8
5	Texas	9	1884	2067	626	3951	6.3	39	439
6	Baylor	9	1625	2162	665	3787	5.7	33	420.8
7	Kansas	9	1546	2076	550	3622	6.6	36	402.4
8	Oklahoma State	9	1091	2361	721	3452	4.8	23	383.6
9	West Virginia	9	1334	2005	636	3339	5.3	29	371
10	Iowa State	9	828	2364	652	3192	4.9	17	354.7

Kansas was the most explosive offense in the league, but they tended towards feast/famine and had more possession issues than Linda Blair in the Exorcist. The schizophrenic Texas offense actually played multiple styles of offense over the course of the year to varying degrees of success. Oklahoma had a good offense on balance, but it was pace dependent, inconsistent and they earned a debilitating goose egg against Texas with Dillon Gabriel out. That queered their season stats considerably.

Texas, Kansas and Oklahoma had the worst times of possession in the Big 12. The knee jerk response to that is to blame the offense (citing complementary football, a phrase talking heads now use often, about 25% of the time correctly) but the fact is that a victimized defense holds the primary responsibility for opponents securing 15 play, 80 yard drives. If you don't want to get hammered on time of possession, make a stop. If you think your offense scoring a touchdown on a 3 play, 80 yard drive is a bad thing because "it hurts time of possession", you have a forest/trees problem.

Kansas State liked a slow pace but finally found their big play upside in the passing game with Will Howard. He unlocked the most underrated big play wide receiver corps in the league with his willingness to grip it and rip it down the field. Is running the ball important for offensive success? Extremely. But within a specific context.

Rushing Offense

Rank	Team	Games	Attempts	Yards	Average	TD	Yards/Game
1	Oklahoma	9	394	1899	4.8	16	211
2	Texas	9	354	1884	5.3	21	209.3
3	Kansas State	10	400	2007	5.0	22	200.7
4	TCU	10	395	1954	4.9	23	195.4
5	Baylor	9	379	1625	4.3	20	180.6
6	Kansas	9	300	1546	5.2	17	171.8
7	Texas Tech	9	378	1525	4.0	19	169.4
8	West Virginia	9	321	1334	4.2	15	148.2
9	Oklahoma State	9	345	1091	3.2	13	121.2
10	Iowa State	9	284	828	2.9	6	92

The most effective offenses in the Big 12 ran the ball well. Not only by volume, but in efficiency per carry. Baylor, Texas Tech, West Virginia, Oklahoma State and Iowa State all struggled and it's not coincidental that they were the league's worst offenses. Was that because they couldn't run the ball per se or is that statistic a consequence of a larger failed offense? Iowa State and Oklahoma State couldn't get over the yards per carry Mendoza line. Remember that college statistics attribute sacks to the rushing game, so per carry efficiency is also a good gauge of pass protection and how quickly the ball gets out from the QB. That college wrinkle makes it a sneaky metric for larger offensive health.

Texas boasting the league's best per carry average is particularly impressive when you consider that Quinn Ewers provided little rushing value, whereas the other good rushing offenses all had considerable help from their quarterback's legs.

Should 2022 running success correlation to wins mean that teams should install the wishbone and immediately profit? No. It actually suggests that the most effective running teams ran well from spread concepts because of their passing games and virtuous circles ensued. It's also a talent function: the league's best rushing teams all started NFL quality running backs. The Big 12 will have a paucity of NFL running backs in 2023.

Passing Offense

Rank	Team	Games	Comp.	Att.	INT	PCT	Yards	Ave.	TD	Yards/Game
1	**Texas Tech**	9	236	391	10	60.4	2563	6.6	16	284.8
2	TCU	10	198	315	4	62.9	2665	8.5	23	266.5
3	Iowa State	9	231	368	11	62.8	2364	6.4	11	262.7
4	Oklahoma State	9	204	376	14	54.3	2361	6.3	10	262.3
5	Oklahoma	9	181	301	8	60.1	2265	7.5	18	251.7
6	Baylor	9	179	286	10	62.6	2162	7.6	13	240.2
7	Kansas State	10	179	284	4	63.0	2391	8.4	20	239.1
8	Kansas	9	156	250	5	62.4	2076	8.3	19	230.7
9	Texas	9	159	272	6	58.5	2067	7.6	18	229.7
10	West Virginia	9	184	315	11	58.4	2005	6.4	14	222.8

Ever since the forward pass became a thing, passing efficiency is the goal – not the empty calories of passing attempts. To that end, Texas Tech is not the "best passing attack in the league" as many analysts opined during their broadcasts. From an efficacy perspective, they were in the bottom half of the league and quite limited in what they did. TCU, Kansas and Kansas State were the real passing game stars in the league and TCU gets the ultimate nod for marrying both volume to high efficiency with limited turnovers. That's why Max Duggan was correctly voted the 2022 Big 12 MVP.

Texas was a middle of the road passing attack, a deceptive and inconsistent average between very good (Oklahoma, West Virginia) and absolutely miserable (Oklahoma State, TCU).

While the rushing statistics are persuasive, they are best understood as a companion to a dangerous or viable passing game. In the absence of the latter, the former is difficult unless you're a service academy. That is the real key to modern football. Can you run it well enough to punish a light or honest box, convert a tough 3rd and 1, or power it in on the goalline for 6 points instead of 3? Do you block well enough to avoid negative plays, thus avoiding perpetually chasing the sticks? In the modern era of football, if a college passing attack isn't averaging over 7.5 yards per attempt, it's hard to actually fulfill the potential of the running game. Understand this and you're a graduate degree level football fan.

QUARTERBACK

Player	Height	Weight	Class
Quinn Ewers	6'2"	204	SO
Charles Wright	6'1"	206	SO
Maalik Murphy	6'5"	235	FR/RS
Arch Manning	6'4"	212	FR

	Comp.	Att.	Pct.	Yards	TD	Int	Rating
Quinn Ewers	172	296	58.1	2177	15	6	132.5

Quinn Ewers had a tumultuous first season at quarterback, his play reminding us that he hadn't played a full season of football since his sophomore year of high school. Age doesn't define the novice, familiarity and experience with the task does. Ewers was a novice. His ill-conceived Ohio State adventure in what should have been his senior year of high school no more gave him quarterbacking experience than being a season ticket holder for the Astros makes you ready to play second base. Last year, Ewers was effectively a true freshman starting quarterback. One deprived of an entire season of high school development. Freshman saviors at the quarterback position have a generally unsatisfying history, but Longhorn fans love nothing more than projecting perfection onto a blank slate with no track record until games get played, holes are revealed and fantasies about the backup begin.

Given that reality, it's fairly amazing that Ewers could successfully throw a forward pass in front of 100,000 people with 300 pound men trying to maim him, much less play average football. Ewers finished the season with a mediocre 132 passing efficiency rating, throwing 15 touchdowns to 6 interceptions while completing just over 58% of his 296 passing attempts at 7.4 yards per attempt in 10 games of action. He was an inaccurate, inconsistent player.

Those mediocre numbers disguised a series of up and down performances in line with what one might expect from a rookie signal caller. Ewers missed most of three games after a shoulder injury against Alabama, a contest where he was slicing and dicing the Tide in early action (9 of 12 for 134 yards). Pro tip: don't jump in the air when a 240 pound linebacker is about to pile drive you. He returned against Oklahoma and destroyed the Sooners, throwing 4 touchdowns behind a well-crafted game plan that exploited a bad Sooner defense that couldn't lay a glove on him in the pocket and forced Brent Venables to take halftime IV quaaludes in hopes of getting his heartbeat under 180.

That was the apogee of the Ewers experience. In the following weeks he was drive-the-bus competent in wins over Iowa State and Kansas State, but his performance fell off of a cliff in losses to Oklahoma State (19 of 49, 3 interceptions) and TCU (17 of 39, 1 interception). Ewers closed out the season wearing training wheels, throwing the ball only 37 times combined in running-game driven wins over Kansas and Baylor. After a month of bowl game preparation, Texas – absent Bijan and Roschon - rolled out a quick-game spread passing attack against Washington that looked a lot like what Ewers did at Southlake Carroll. Ewers played well, going 31 of 47 for 369 yards and no turnovers in that loss.

The only way through is forward. In the offseason, Ewers cut his trademark mullet to signal a more businesslike approach and worked to get into the best shape of his life, adding muscle while losing fat. Consequently, he now moves better in the pocket and will be able to better protect himself from hits. Quinn will also grow in his understanding of the offense, allowing Texas to get into and out of plays at the line of scrimmage. The ecosystem around him will also be better. Texas has upgraded the receiving room markedly, returns all five starters on the offensive line and has built out depth at nearly every position. For added motivation, he has some very talented backups breathing down his neck at practice every day. Sark will keep the offense multiple, but expect more traditional spread looks, which is Ewers' default comfort zone.

Part of what made Ewers beguiling as a recruit was his knack for releasing the ball accurately from a dizzying variety of arm angles and different platforms. The downside of that is that Ewers never developed a base throwing motion that he could fall back on when he just needed to deliver the correct ball on time in rhythm with the offense. That lack of a base platform particularly plagues quarterbacks who are hurt, confused or pressured. Perhaps the most interesting development of the offseason will be whether Ewers can develop a core foundational throwing motion that he can improvise off of, rather than making the improvisation itself his foundation. If he does, Texas should have a much more consistent offense and Ewers will see his numbers go from up and down to up and upper.

Maalik Murphy finally got healthy enough to show Longhorn fans what Steve Sarkisian saw in the young California product, dominating the Spring game before thousands of Longhorn fans. Before his first throws, casual fans probably wondered why Texas had a defensive end playing quarterback. The redshirt freshman is a massive, strong athlete with elite velocity that helps make up for his inexperience in recognition. He was most comfortable in set piece offense where he knew his progressions and could cut the field in half. In that scrimmage, Murphy dropped consecutive deep dimes attacking #39, walk-on cornerback Ja'Faar Johnson, one of them dropped by DeAndre Moore, the other housed by Johntay Cook for a 79 yard touchdown. That helped pad the stat line to an impressive 9 of 13 for 165 yards, but he also had some receiver drops and his more mundane throws were actually his most impressive. Murphy's massive 6-5, 235+ pound frame exudes strength in the pocket and he's athletic enough to move his platform around. Good luck getting him on the ground without a clean shot and multiple tacklers. Texas can win games with Murphy at quarterback and he will continue to progress even more with a healthy summer and Fall camp. Murphy was contacted by FBS programs after his Spring game to test his interest, but the hope is that Murphy will continue to develop under the staff that believed in him with the understanding that he will get a fair shake in the post-Ewers quarterback competition.

Arch Manning was a gigantic recruiting get for the Longhorns as a validation of Sark's coaching and the Longhorn program in general, but also because Arch the prospect is pretty darn good, too. The grandson of Archie and nephew of Peyton and Eli, Manning comes from football royalty, but coaches and program observers are impressed with his humble demeanor, football IQ and competitiveness. He throws a nice ball as well. Unlike Peyton and Eli, Arch inherited grandpa's athleticism and pairs that with his uncle's big frames. Manning is a pocket passer first and foremost, but he is mobile, runs well and will play his ball at every bit of 6-4, 225 when it's his time in Austin. When will it be his time in Austin? When he's ready and wins the job. Sarkisian doesn't really do coronations, Maalik Murphy has his own ideas about who should succeed Quinn Ewers, and the Manning family are football sophisticated, understanding that pressing Arch into early action to satisfy media demands is ruinous to his development. Manning doesn't need to start four years to go to the NFL. Naturally, it didn't take long for naysayers and click seekers to proclaim Arch a bust after his Spring game throwing to walk-ons with no blocking when he should have been getting ready for Isidore Newman's prom. Ignore the noise and chatter around Manning and realize that the NFL doesn't have a single quarterback who was fully formed at 18 years old.

Charles Wright is a redshirt sophomore. The depth chart insurance policy showed a live arm in high school at Austin High a few miles from the Longhorn campus, but limited action in open practice environments shows that he has a ways to go.

Prognosis

The 2022 Spring game didn't settle the University of Texas quarterback controversy between Hudson Card and Quinn Ewers, but the 2023 Spring game was a confirmation of what the informed already knew: Quinn Ewers is the Longhorn starting quarterback. The real drama happened at backup quarterback. Recruiting enthusiasts and national media had already elevated Arch Manning to the second team, poised to take over as a true freshman the first time that Ewers threw an incompletion against Rice.

At least that was the fantasy for a certain weird subset that dwells in the bowels of internet message boards or have ESPN hot take shows. The reality is that Maalik Murphy showed why he had been the talk of camp and Arch Manning showed why healthy football programs don't put true freshmen early enrollees in their two deep. If Quinn Ewers' offseason development sets the offensive ceiling at Texas, Maalik Murphy's progress sets the floor. Football is a violent game and the expectation that your starting quarterback could miss a game or three is not improbable bad luck, but a sizable likelihood. The takeaway from the spring and summer is that Texas has two improved quarterbacks — one clearly the starter — who can win games and an impressive prospect waiting in the wings behind them. Juggling talent in the world of short attention spans, TikTok timelines and portal tampering is no easy feat, but the current snapshot for the Texas Longhorns is very good and only getting better.

RUNNING BACK

Player	Height	Weight	Class
Keilan Robinson	5'9"	185	SR
Jonathon Brooks	6'0"	204	SO
Savion Red	5'10"	214	SO
Jaydon Blue	6'0"	191	SO
CJ Baxter	6'1"	210	FR
Tre Wisner	5'11"	180	FR

| | Rushing | | | | Receiving | | | |
	Att	Yds	Avg	TD	Rec	Yds	Avg	TD
Keilan Robinson	25	94	3.4	0	20	219	10.9	3
Jonathan Brooks	30	204	6.6	5	2	37	18.5	1
Jaydon Blue	15	35	2.2	0	0	0	0	0
Savion Red	0	0	0	0	6	34	5.7	1

Jonathon Brooks is good at ghosting tacklers, but the way he spells his first name will never evade spell check. Brooks has a gliding deceptive running style that seems to suggest a lack of speed and explosiveness but that isn't borne out by on-field results. Brooks brings to mind John Wooden's wisdom that one should be quick, but not hurry. Over two years of spot action, Brooks has totaled 340 yards rushing on 51 carries with 6 touchdowns and he added a 34 yard touchdown catch in the Alamo Bowl against Washington. Brooks will be first in line in a deep running back room and while replacing the elite duo of Bijan Robinson and Roschon Johnson is no easy task, the third year record-breaking runner from Hallettsville has the potential to be a fine replacement. If the offensive line and supporting cast levels up as it should, #24 might have an impressive coming-out party. Brooks' slashing upright running style is difficult to convey without seeing it, but he is capable of making smooth cuts and his versatility and capabilities as a receiver and pass blocker cinch his starting role. No other runner on the roster can stay on the field for every game

scenario like Brooks can and that fact alone makes him the clear #1. Whether Brooks is a bell cow or simply first man in the rotation will depend on his play and how many mouths Sark's offense wants to feed.

Keilan Robinson transferred to the 40 Acres from Alabama two years ago and the Washington DC area athlete has unique quickness, which he has evidenced as a runner and as the premier punt blocker in the conference. Last year, Robinson added to his special teams tally by running in a blocked punt for a touchdown while averaging 25.2 yards per kickoff return as the team's best returner. Robinson also had an intriguing evolution as a pass catcher, nabbing 20 balls for 219 yards and 3 touchdowns. If Keilan can expand his acumen even more this year, he will be a major asset in the passing game. Over two years, Robinson has also chipped in 408 yards rushing at 5.8 yards per carry. The versatile Robinson is an unselfish member of a crowded running back room and his willingness to star on special teams highlights the sort of team-first attitude that endears him to Texas fans and staff.

CJ Baxter comes to Texas as the #1 running back prospect in the nation. The Floridian dominated at Edgewater high school and unlike so many other running back products from the state of Texas who arrive with a lot of time already logged in the weight room, Baxter still has physical upside with a corresponding learning curve. Baxter is currently listed at 210 pounds but he will play his best ball twenty pounds north of that. A naturally powerful athlete, Baxter also has terrific hands out of the backfield. Baxter is an efficient runner who doesn't waste movement and he has a knack for breaking long runs despite his size. Pad level has to improve, but college linebackers will teach him that lesson. This offseason will be important for him to learn his assignments and gain the trust of coaches that he can do more than just tote the rock. A running back that can't credibly block for Quinn Ewers when asked to will limit their playing time.

Jaydon Blue saw action last year in mop up duty, but he had a fine Spring scrimmage that highlighted a renewed willingness to run inside despite his 190 pound frame. Blue is a gifted athlete and whether the 2nd year runner has the patience to wait and earn his opportunities remains to be seen.

Savion Red converted from wide receiver to running back and the thickly built athlete took to his new position like a duck to water. The compact 215 pounder has great hands and he runs with power. He may already be the best short yardage runner currently on the roster. Red's primary governor on upside is his approach to football and how seriously he takes his responsibilities off of the field.

Tre Wisner was employed in high school as an all purpose back and is equally comfortable as a receiver or runner. Wisner totaled 210 yards of offense in the state title game, scoring twice through the air in DeSoto's win over Austin Vandegrift. Eventually converting to wide receiver is not out of the question, but for now he is a running back with a strong 3rd down skill set.

Prognosis

The Horns have six scholarship running backs on the roster, but Robinson and Brooks are the only two with meaningful experience. Given Brooks' versatility, he is the closest thing that the team has to an every down back who can play in any game context. Expect Texas to integrate CJ Baxter into the lineup, but early contests like Bama and Baylor on the road may highlight the veteran runners while Baxter gets comfortable, learns the offense and is set up for a more active second half of the season. Red and Blue are talented, but both primary colors need to earn the staff's trust. Tre Wisner will almost certainly redshirt. Realistically, Texas should expect to lose 2-3 current running backs by year end; Keilan Robinson to graduation with at least one or two transfers out.

The overall talent level here is pretty good, but the unit's upside will rest on Brooks becoming a reliable 1,000+ yard type rusher, Keilan Robinson continuing his growth as a pass catcher and getting CJ Baxter integrated into the lineup after a big offseason in the weight room and in the dining hall.

WIDE RECEIVER

Player	Height	Weight	Class
Jordan Whittington	6'1"	205	SR
Isaiah Neyor	6'3"	216	SR
Xavier Worthy	6'1"	164	JR
Adonai Mitchell	6'4"	195	JR
Casey Cain	6'3"	196	SO
Johntay Cook II	6'0"	184	FR
DeAndre Moore Jr.	6'0"	192	FR
Ryan Niblett	5'10"	174	FR

	Receiving				Rushing			
	Rec	Yds	Avg	TD	Att	Yds	Avg	TD
Xavier Worthy	60	760	12.7	9	2	14	7	0
Jordan Whittington	50	652	13	1	0	0	0	0
Casey Cain	8	201	25.1	0	0	0	0	0

Xavier Worthy had a sophomore slump last year. That is if being the team's leading receiver while catching 60 balls for 760 yards and 9 touchdowns can be considered a letdown. Given Worthy's extraordinary gifts and the sky high expectations around him, it qualifies. The skinny junior from Fresno struggled badly to connect on deep balls all season after being thrust into the role of the team's only viable deep threat while carrying double duty as the clear #1 target in the passing game. At times, Worthy was over targeted and over-burdened in roles to which he was not accustomed and it showed. No real blame to cast. It simply was how the season unfolded after some key injuries and some other players could not step up. While Xavier is extremely durable for his size, 165 pound pass catchers have a pitch count just like any skill player.

It was revealed after the season that Worthy was playing with a broken hand, which helped explain a 11% drop percentage. That does not explain his sudden inability to track deep balls. Statistically, his sophomore year was a considerable step down from Worthy's dominant freshman campaign, where he earned 1st Team All-Big 12 honors and set Longhorn

freshmen receiving records for receptions (62), yardage (981), and touchdowns (12). Still, this is a player entering his 3rd year on campus who already has 21 career touchdown catches (and has thrown for another) and is generally regarded as the scariest 1-on-1 matchup in the league.

A much better supporting cast and better experience at quarterback will allow Worthy to return to his traditional role as a Z receiver who is at his best after-the-catch. In 2023, expect a major return to form. Worthy had a strong spring and he has demonstrated further advancements as a route runner and his elite quickness has not dissipated. Xavier Worthy will be one of the premier receivers in the country and the straw that stirs the drink for what should be the best receiving corps in the Big 12 conference.

Adonai A.D. Mitchell has been the talk of the offseason. The 6-4 greyhound lean transfer from Georgia blew away coaches and teammates in the spring with his body control and catch radius. Program insiders have upped their predictions of Mitchell from quality starting receiver to potential star; several sources believe that he is already one of the best handful of players on the team. Mitchell is a Missouri City, Texas native and a classic late bloomer, not only in terms of his football experience and skill development, but also in his physical composition. He grew another two inches post high school at Georgia and he's still filling out his lithe frame. His speed, play strength and overall durability will all improve as he gets stronger over summer workouts. That's a priority for him this offseason and it has to occur in the cafeteria as much as the weight room. Mitchell needs to eat with the offensive line three times a week after lifting and develop some armor.

Mitchell saw extensive early playing time at Georgia as a true freshman (29 catches, 426 yards, 4 touchdowns) on their 2021 national championship team. After his promising freshman season, Mitchell's injury plagued sophomore season was nearly a wash except for the opener and some late season playoff appearances where he was not in ideal football shape. He played only 130 snaps. The primary culprit was a pesky high ankle sprain followed by an undisclosed thumb injury. So his season was reduced to a 4 catch, 65 yard and 1 touchdown performance against Oregon in the opener and another two touchdowns cumulatively against Ohio State and TCU in the playoffs. Mitchell has scored 7 touchdowns at Georgia on only 38 career catches and he was not particularly open on four of them. He just takes the ball away. Mitchell is a touchdown maker, intermediate chain mover and potential pass interference magnet. Mitchell's magical power is that he can maintain his stride running full speed while he rotates his upper body and plucks the ball. That's a great asset and a major irritant to defensive backs in otherwise good coverage. Durability is the big question mark for Mitchell. That's hard to handicap, but getting stronger always helps. A healthy Mitchell makes the Longhorn receiver room the league's best.

Isaiah Neyor was last year's A.D. Mitchell before being derailed by a preseason knee injury that forced him to miss the entire 2022 season. A classic overlooked dark horse recruit, the Arlington native came to football late in life and then saw his 2020 prepster recruiting evaluations handicapped by COVID disruptions. Neyor went to Laramie, Wyoming where he earned All-Conference honors in his second season, catching 44 balls for 878 yards and 12 touchdowns despite rather poor Cowboy quarterback play. Neyor caught eight touchdowns over his last six games and he accounted for an amazing 41.5% of Wyoming's passing offense overall. The 6-3, 215 pound Neyor's trademark is a deceptive change-of-pace and the ability to win balls downfield with a terrific catch radius, sticky hands, and good adjustments to the football. He is a tracker, not a blazer, but accurate ball radar and the ability to win in tight spaces is one of the most important aspects of wide receiver play. Since arriving on campus, Neyor has impressed with better than anticipated athleticism, size, and a much wider skill set than was first perceived. Unfortunately, a torn ACL in Fall camp robbed the Longhorn offense of their starting X receiver and Neyor was robbed of a home state debut where he would have served as the team's top deep threat. Neyor's rehab has gone well and he has been running at full speed; whether he's back at 75% or 100% and can play through contact is to be determined.

Jordan Whittington made the most important catch of his career when he finally caught a break. Before the 2022 season, the talented Cuero product experienced an unending succession of injuries that upended his developmental trajectory and sapped his explosive running style. Before last season, Whittington had only played in 14 total games over three years due to injuries, after losing his entire freshman season to a hernia. Whittington rehabbed, worked on his body, finally caught some luck and played in all 13 games last year while totaling 50 catches for 652 yards.

The bodied up 6-1, 205 pound Whittington also won the title as the best blocking wide receiver in the Big 12, amassing a highlight reel of blocks on manhandled defensive backs. Whittington is a wonderful complement to Mitchell, Neyor and Worthy, fully capable of punishing a defense for overplaying dynamic outside threats, in addition to being a reliable chain mover. His blocking, maturity and team-first mentality are a welcome balance to a room where every member wants the ball on every play.

Casey Cain was a lightly recruited prospect from Louisiana but the long-limbed wideout worked his way into the 2022 rotation after Neyor's injury, catching 8 balls for 201 yards, including a 4 catch, 108 yard performance in the Alamo Bowl. The 3rd year sophomore lacks explosiveness, but he is a smooth route runner with long arms and is still growing into his frame. He wasn't capable of serving as a viable #3 receiver last year, but with another year of development, he should be a valuable member of the rotation.

DeAndre Moore is a freshman wideout who plays the game with a maturity and reliability that belies his years. A fine route runner, Moore had a couple of drops in the Spring game but carried on unflustered to finish with six catches. He will see rotational snaps and provide depth.

Johntay Cook is a true freshman from DeSoto who is already demonstrating high level ball skills and route running. He is quicker than fast, but that's because his quickness is elite.

Ryan Niblett is a true freshman and his game is less sophisticated and refined than his 2023 class peers Cook and Moore, but Niblett offers RPMs and elite football speed. He ran a 10.4 100 meters and 21.25 200 meters as a high school junior and every bit of that translates to the gridiron.

Prognosis

Texas will have the best starting receivers in the Big 12 and should boast a top ten unit nationally if the gods of health were sufficiently placated by the burnt offerings of Quinn Ewers' mullet and beard. The importance of avoiding injury can't be overstated for this unit given that Sark prefers not to carry dead roster weight at receiver and wants all of them engaged and involved in the rotation getting meaningful practice reps. The Horns have an eight man room, three of them true freshmen. Troy Omeire, Brenen Thompson and Jaden Alexis transferred out. C'est la vie. Don't be surprised if Cook, Moore, Niblett and Cain all get plenty of work in camp and in the early season to sort out their reliability, even as Sark channels most of the passing game to the core four of Worthy, Mitchell, Whittington and

Neyor. Placing Neyor and Mitchell on early season pitch counts to preserve them for the whole season may also be advisable.

New wide receivers coach Chris Jackson is a technician and the group should exhibit better chemistry with Quinn Ewers in Year 2, particularly as he rewards the players who read coverages correctly and get to the right spots. The floor for this group is pretty good, but the ceiling for this unit with a revitalized Neyor and a healthy Adonai Mitchell is sky high.

TIGHT END

Player	Height	Weight	Class
Patrick Bayouth	6'4"	277	SR
Ja'Tavion Sanders	6'4"	241	JR
Gunnar Helm	6'5"	251	JR
Juan Davis	6'4"	221	JR
Spencer Shannon	6'7"	240	FR
Will Randle	6'2"	225	FR

| | Receiving | | | | | Rushing | | | |
	Rec	Yds	Avg	TD		Att	Yds	Avg	TD
Ja'Tavion Sanders	54	613	11.4	5					
Gunner Helm	5	44	8.8	0					

Ja'Tavion Sanders is the most talented tight end at Texas since Jermichael Finley. Sanders debuted last year with 54 catches, 613 yards and 5 touchdowns, earning 1st Team All Big 12 honors. Sanders also revealed himself to be a competent blocker in all phases, though with room for improvement. Still, Sanders' willing blocking was a pleasant surprise for a player perceived as a flex receiving tight end, With quality receivers providing deep and intermediate threats around him and occupying defensive gravity, the sure-handed Sanders can be used as a chess piece to hunt opportunistic matchups against slower linebackers or smallish safeties. Sanders is a good athlete, but not a physical freak.

His athleticism is more subtle, built on body control, ease of lateral movement, overall coordination. Anytime you have a mobile 6-4, 240 pound target with great hands surrounded by a high level receiving corps, getting open isn't a particularly difficult task. Texas fans should enjoy Sanders' junior campaign because he will be in the NFL at this time next year.

Gunnar Helm will be the #2 tight end. The big Coloradan from Cherry Creek is improving as a pass catcher and blocker and he possesses good feet for a 6-5, 250+ pound athlete. The former high school flex tight end will continue to improve as a blocker as he gets stronger and bigger and is considered the 2nd most reliable tight end on the roster. Given a fairly shallow receiving room, Sarkisian won't be shy about employing two tight end sets to hunt for certain coverages or attack defenses that choose to go with light personnel.

Juan Davis has Juan in a million versatility as a former all-district quarterback in high school, but hasn't been able to employ his athleticism on the field as a tweener. He needs to gain weight and spend more time in the playbook.

Freshman **Spencer Shannon** is a skyscraper tight end who is still growing and is rumored to already be 6-8, 240. He was primarily a blocker at Mater Dei.

Will Randle was Arch Manning's #1 target in high school and the undersized but flypaper handed tight end will need a few years to build his body up for the college game.

Walk-on **Patrick Bayouth** saw extensive snaps in the Spring game as a blocking tight end. Whether that was a function of the freshmen tight ends not yet arriving on campus or the coaches rewarding his play, the 6-4, 280 pound defensive conversion could provide some needed blocking bulk in certain sets.

Prognosis

Texas spent 35% of its snaps last year with two tight ends on the field, ranking them in the Top 5 of college football. That's a bigger number than Sark likely wanted, but a thin receiver corps, a young offensive line that needed help simplifying gap responsibilities and a quarterback who needed the option of additional pass protectors to simplify his responsibilities forced it. Expect that number to decrease if the wide receiver room remains healthy and as the coaches gain confidence in Ewers' game management.

The Longhorn tight end room has a marquee headliner in JT Sanders and a passable #2 in Gunnar Helm. Juan Davis has tantalizing physical potential, but hasn't yet put it together and still hasn't gained the weight necessary to be an effective blocker. The rest of the room is composed of freshmen and a preferred walk-on, who could see situational snaps at best. Expect Sark to use Sanders and Helm extensively in the offense, even as he seeks to move the unit to more traditional spread looks that allow Ewers to take advantage of his skill set and for the Longhorn receivers to attack more areas of the field.

OFFENSIVE LINE

Player	Height	Weight	Class
Christian Jones	6'6"	322	SR
Hayden Conner	6'5"	314	JR
Jake Majors	6'3"	308	JR
Sawyer Goram-Welch	6'4"	307	JR
DJ Campbell	6'3"	332	SO
Kelvin Banks Jr.	6'5"	318	SO
Cameron Williams	6'5"	360	SO
Cole Hutson	6'5"	314	SO
Max Merril	6'4"	297	SO
Neto Umeozulu	6'4"	325	FR/RS
Malik Agbo	6'4"	312	FR/RS
Conner Robertson	6'4"	314	FR/RS
Jaydon Chatman	6'4"	299	FR
Connor Stroh	6'7"	365	FR
Andre Cojoe	6'6"	358	FR
Payton Kirkland	6'6"	367	FR
Trevor Goosby	6'6"	275	FR

Kelvin Banks was a revelation in his freshman season, starting all 13 games for the Longhorns at left tackle. Aside from the rarity of college freshmen being useful starters anywhere, much less the offensive line, starting one at left tackle is nearly suicidal to an offense. Banks turned in the most impressive true freshman offensive tackle performance in Longhorn history, earning 2nd team All-Big 12 honors from the coaches and freshman All-American accolades from multiple outlets. Those plaudits undersell the quality of his play. He acquitted himself well against Alabama's Will Anderson, more than held his own against Iowa State's Will McDonald and won his matchup against Kansas State's Felix Anudike-Uzomah. All three of those edge players were 1st round NFL draft picks. Banks possesses excellent feet and good technique, but his competitive determination and seriousness about football are unmatched. Kelvin rarely makes mental errors and his effort is unrelenting. Banks was a spectacular pass protector in 2022. Per Pro Football Focus, his 3.5% pressure rate allowed on true pass sets ranked sixth among all Power Five tackles. His pass-block efficiency score was also second among Big 12 tackles, behind only Sooner

senior Anton Harrison – another 1st round draft pick. Banks is a willing run blocker with the agility to dominate smaller defenders, but a lack of experience and time in the weight room means that he occasionally struggles to move bigger defenders at the point of attack. That should improve and his pass blocking acumen is not a perishable skill. Banks is one of the Top 10 offensive tackles in college football and a future 1st round NFL draft pick.

Christian Jones' returns for his 6th year in Austin and the right tackle has 35 career starts under his belt. Christian's career has been an exercise in patience. Patience from the coaches and the fanbase for his failings as a pass protector and patience from Christian to stop beating himself by abandoning fundamentals. Over 1,411 total snaps played as a sophomore and junior, Jones allowed 34 hurries, 7 quarterback hits and 9 sacks while playing right and left tackle. In 2022, Jones played a career high 811 snaps and allowed only 9 hurries, no quarterback hits and 3 sacks. That is a considerable improvement and whether a function of maturation, consistent coaching, or increased comfort, it's a good bet that this positive trend line will continue into his final season and third season playing right tackle.

Jones still allows too many inside free runs from outside defenders, but he has learned to trust his enormous strength and length and rarely lunges anymore. Despite his histori-

cal pass blocking woes, Jones is a good, sometimes devastating, run blocker. There are numerous highlights of #70 driving defenders 10-15 yards downfield and the 330 pounder will add to that collection in 2023. Remember that Jones did not play football until his junior year of high school, preferring soccer. His slow growth into a quality offensive tackle happened in the spotlight as a starter whereas in a healthier program those growing pains would have been hidden at practice while he incubated. Jones successfully weathered some tough moments early in his career and he has a high probability of earning postseason accolades. He and Kelvin Banks make a formidable tackle tandem, likely the league's best.

Fourth year junior center **Jake Majors** has notched 27 starts as a Longhorn and the two time Academic 1st Team All-Big 12 selection excelled last year as a pass blocker, but he struggled as a run blocker and the 23 point delta between his Pro Focus Football grade in each measure is testament to that fact. Majors is not particularly powerful at the point of contact, but he has active feet and he is good at coordinating line calls. He's also agile enough to act as a puller from the center position. Majors can struggle to hold up against powerful nose tackles on interior run plays and the staff has experimented with getting more size and power inside, but injury, unsuitability, or need in other areas short circuited those attempts. Odds are that Majors will remain a stabilizing piece for the Texas line, but expect Cole Hutson to see more work at center in August. If he can duplicate Majors' leadership while providing more power in the inside running game, Texas could see a shift.

Hayden Conner fits Kyle Flood's preferred size requirements for Big Humans nicely. In fact, he fits the size requirements for the protagonist in a Godzilla movie. Conner started 13 games at left guard last year and he had some ups and downs in his first year as a starter. A penchant for offsides penalties and not maintaining blocks were the major downs. This offseason, Conner committed to losing a few pounds to increase his agility and the twenty pound weight loss and general redistribution has proven beneficial. Given the excellent class of young offensive linemen behind him, Hayden needs to perform better as a run blocker (he had a particularly rough outing against Alabama) and continue his overall maturation. Last year, there was discussion of trying him at center as the coaches love his size and intellect there, but the coaches won't pull the trigger on that move from any starting guard on the roster until they're positive that the shift creates upgrades at both center and guard. Given his ability to move mass around the field, it is unsurprising that Conner is a Physics major.

Cole Hutson was the sole early enrollee for the much hyped 2022 offensive line class and less heralded than several of his peers, but he earned a starting job at right guard over older more established players. If Hutson was supposed to be the high floor program guy that the coaches bring along slowly, the physical young guard from Frisco did not get that memo. Hutson started 13 games as a true freshman and while he had some real struggles and didn't exhibit Kelvin Banks level ability - who does? – he proved himself a gutty and game competitor playing through injury while earning valuable experience. Immediately after the season, Hutson had surgery on a torn labrum that prevented him from going through spring practice. He also played in the bowl game with a lingering knee injury sustained against Baylor that required him to be carted off of the field. There may be more talented offensive linemen on campus, but good luck finding one tougher. Anyone who beats him out at right guard will have to earn it.

Cam Williams is noticeably big on an offensive line of giants. The 6-5, 360 pound tackle from Duncanville is massive but has surprising athletic ability for his size. Williams has reshaped his body, but he has a bit more to go to eliminate some stiffness and reach his full potential. Right now, Williams is the 3rd offensive tackle, but Texas coaches are willing to play him at guard as well. They may even dabble with throwing a tight end number on him. Expect Williams to play at least 250 snaps this year as the staff prepares him for an inevitable starting role down the road.

DJ Campbell played in seven games last year and the powerfully built guard was a former 5 star recruit. Campbell is immensely strong, but he needs time to learn his assignments and grasp the nuances of the offense and his position. Pass blocking needs to be a particular point of emphasis. If Campbell can't win a job this August, he should see heavy rotational play. If the Longhorns make significant shifts to their three returning starters inside at center or either guard spot, Campbell's development will likely have been the driving force. Keep your attention on practice reports.

Malik Agbo is another member of the heralded 2022 offensive line class. The redshirt freshman was strategically held back to spread out the class a bit more and lengthen his developmental timeline.

Connor Robertson missed the spring with wrist and shoulder injuries, but the staff like him as the future at center.

Neto Umeozulu is a redshirt freshman from Allen who still has plenty of meat left on the developmental bone. He moves very well for his size and the staff likes his long term trajectory at guard or tackle. Expect Umeozulu to force his way into being given some snaps and of Flood's core rotation guys.

Sawyer Gorham-Welch is a 4th year junior still adjusting to his move from a packed defensive line room to guard last year. Intense competition by virtue of twelve big bodies being added to the unit in the last two classes means that Gorham-Welch must adapt or fall behind.

Max Merril needs seasoning and a lot of time in the weight room.

The 2023 offensive line class is not as heralded as the 2022 group, but the five man class is even more gigantic, featuring Kyle Flood's largest assortment of humans yet. **Jaydon Chatman**, **Trevor Goosby**, **Payton Kirkland**, **Connor Stroh** and **Andre Cojoe** will all compete to be on the two deep, but the smart money says that most of them will redshirt and start the seasoning process. Flood needs to balance playing his best on the two deep with spreading out eligibility timelines.

Prognosis

The Texas offensive line will be improved from last year. A safe prediction given the return of five starters with a combined 101 collective starts and two bookend tackles who will compete for conference (Jones) and national (Banks) accolades. The interior offensive line should see intense Fall camp competition and has the greatest uncertainty. That makes sense as the interior requires the biggest step up in play. Flood may continue with his established inside troika from last year, allowing another year of experience and S&C to grow their capabilities or he may experiment and start trying to find upgrades and combinations that result in a superior overall unit. There is no easy answer and his options will be largely informed by the development of players like Campbell, Williams and Umeozulu and how Cole Hutson auditions at both center and guard.

The Longhorn staff has done a fine job restocking the cupboard on the recruiting trail, but Texas fans must remain patient with the normal human offensive linemen who aren't on the accelerated Kelvin Banks developmental timeline. Pointing to a phenom and asking why the rest of the young players aren't doing that is like pointing to Led Zeppelin and asking why your local cover band can't sell out arenas. Most college offensive linemen don't start to peak until their fourth year in the program and players like Christian Jones prove it may take even longer. The key is having the right bodies, intense competition, a judicious use of redshirts and continuity in coaching.

Defining Good Defense In Modern Football

One of the merits of getting a full conference slate of results in a round robin format is that it allows apples to apples comparisons. Well, not quite apples to apples, but at least it's apple to crabapples instead of apples to lasagna. Limited conference universes are not true apples to apples because Iowa State's defense never had the good fortune of playing Iowa State's offense and the Kansas Jayhawks were spared getting lit up by their own offense. Injuries can also have an impact. Texas received a major statistical favor by not having to face Dillon Gabriel in Dallas, which would have turned a 49-0 utter demolition into a more conventional 56-28 woodshedding.

Nonetheless, round robins provide very useful data because they throw out questionable non-conference opponents and forces like against like. We also care more about what happens in our conference ecosystem in general. Baylor's defense dominated non-con opponents Albany and Texas State while the Longhorn defense faced potent non-con offenses like Alabama and UTSA. The idea that we can still glean data from these contests for comparison with the right statistical boundaries is fraught. Yes, even if you "adjust" for strength. You can't do it very well — even if the stat heads imply they can. Which they even acknowledge by throwing out FCS results vs FBS teams.

There's also nothing to be gained comparing whether a good team blew out a really bad team 48-7 or 62-7. The human mind still wants to see the latter score result as more dominant. Football doesn't work that way. Playing weak non-conference opponents, in combination with preseason hype, fuels false perceptions that still carry into November and December. And even into postseason All Big 12 selections (ahem).

So let's make the data dance, add a little context, and see what we see. We'll start the big picture with scoring defense and then narrow our focus...

Scoring Defense

Rank	Team	Games	TD	FG	XPT	2XP	PTS	Avg/Game
1	Texas	9	25	9	23	1	204	22.7
2	Kansas State	10	28	13	21	2	232	23.2
3	Iowa State	9	27	9	27	0	216	24.0
4	TCU	10	33	10	33	0	261	26.1
5	Baylor	9	35	10	32	0	276	30.7
6	Oklahoma State	9	35	13	33	1	284	31.6
7	Texas Tech	9	34	16	33	1	287	31.9
8	Oklahoma	9	42	11	38	1	325	36.1
9	Kansas	9	43	12	39	2	339	37.7
10	West Virginia	9	43	13	39	1	340	37.8

Hey, points on the board is all that matters, right? Sort of.

Scoring defense is a **team measure**, predominantly influenced by your defense. That subtle distinction is important. Scoring defense is a decent shorthand, but it can be incredibly deceptive, such as when the defense being measured is saddled with a turnover prone offense or poor special teams play. Meanwhile, Hurry-Up-No-Huddle spread teams have defenses that may have to defend as many as fifteen possessions in a game. One must adjust for pace and possessions. The Air Force Academy plays pretty good defense, but not as well as their gross statistics imply. They have games where they might have to defend against only seven offensive possessions. Having to play very little defense is a great way of playing good scoring defense.

Last year, the Texas defense handled Baylor's offense, but the Bears scored a safety and a defensive touchdown to fuel a 27 point total that suggested a solid offensive effort to the casual box score scanner. That's not really what happened though. The Texas defense clearly won their matchup. For a more dramatic example, see TCU's 62-14 decimation of Iowa State. A Frog track meet, right? Not really. TCU had less than 400 yards of offense and averaged 5.5 yards per play. The Cyclone offense and special teams played poor "team defense" and kept giving the Frogs touchdowns and short fields.

Points per game allowed generally does a solid job of identifying the middling to worst defenses as pure volume doesn't lie, but it does a poor job of differentiating the elite. And a one game outlier can really skew the data.

Let's talk about per play efficiency instead.

Defensive Yardage

Rank	Team	Games	Rush	Pass	Plays	Yards	Av/Play	TD	AV/Game
1	Iowa State	9	1108	1616	551	2724	4.9	25	302.7
2	Texas	9	1084	2219	676	3303	4.9	24	367.0
3	TCU	10	1641	2246	715	3887	5.4	32	388.7
4	Kansas State	10	1551	2377	692	3928	5.7	27	392.8
5	Baylor	9	1399	2174	621	3573	5.8	33	397.0
6	Texas Tech	9	1749	2344	664	4093	6.2	32	454.8
7	West Virginia	9	1607	2548	650	4155	6.4	41	461.7
8	Oklahoma State	9	1722	2438	698	4160	6.0	35	462.2
9	Kansas	9	1919	2402	701	4321	6.2	43	480.1
10	Oklahoma	9	1913	2555	740	4468	6.0	42	496.4

Now we're drilling down closer to the truth. Notice that the top four performers from points per game remain near the top (albeit in different order) while the middle and bottom remain depressed. Gross yards per game allowed is a useful but deceptive metric. Look instead to yards allowed per play. Texas and Iowa State were the clear conference standouts at 4.9 yards per play with a clear separation from the rest of the league. TCU – the next closest team – is a half yard away. The rest of the league hovers around 6 yards per play. On this basis, the Kansas State defense comes down to earth vs. their points allowed per game metric (remember, offensive pace, special teams and their lack of offensive turnovers helped Wildcat "team defense") while TCU looks better than is popularly perceived. Oklahoma State may be shocking to see at 6.0 yards per play allowed. The Cowboys had only one defensive competency. . . getting off of the field.

Opponent 3rd Down Conversions

Rank	Team	Games	Conv	Att	PCT
1	Oklahoma State	9	39	138	28.3
2	Iowa State	9	36	118	30.5
3	TCU	10	48	147	32.7
4	Kansas State	10	51	140	36.4
5	Texas	9	57	146	39.0
6	Texas Tech	9	58	139	41.7
7	Oklahoma	9	63	148	42.6
8	West Virginia	9	56	126	44.4
9	Kansas	9	68	134	50.7
10	Baylor	9	61	116	52.6

Opponent 4th Down Conversions

Rank	Team	Games	Conv	Att	PCT
1	Texas Tech	9	8	22	36.4
2	Kansas State	10	11	27	40.7
3	Baylor	9	5	12	41.7
4	TCU	10	15	31	48.4
5	Oklahoma State	9	13	25	52.0
6	West Virginia	9	13	21	61.9
7	Texas	9	17	27	63.0
8	Oklahoma	9	13	20	65.0
9	Iowa State	9	8	12	66.7
10	Kansas	9	16	22	72.7

A poor Oklahoma State defense was fantastic at getting off of the field on 3rd down. In fact, you will never see a larger spread between a defense's ability to get off of the field in elite fashion to hemorrhaging big plays and yards on other downs. Former defensive coordinator Derek Mason was great at honing in on key downs while consistently getting whipped outside of them. It's a bizarre asymmetry, but a useful one for the Cowboys. It's the primary reason they upset a better Longhorn football team in Stillwater. Texas went an atrocious 3/19 on 3rd and 4th down combined.

Iowa State was predictably great in this metric and TCU also excelled. Credit TCU's success to a good secondary and smart blitzing while Iowa State is a triumph of team concept defense. The Cyclones also have an underrated strength: every starting defender was at least average and most of them were above average to good. Otherwise good defenses pay an outsized cost for starting just one or two weak links that offenses can pick on. Texas improved here over the course of the season, but this was the clear Achilles heel of the Longhorn defense and a primary contributor to losses to Texas Tech and Oklahoma State. Combine 3rd down with the miserable 4th down numbers for Texas and you have a statistical understanding of how the Horns faltered on the road against an overrated offense like Tech. The Texas defense repeatedly surrendered the only thing that the Red Raider could credibly do on money downs and they never corrected the problem. Texas got better on key downs as the season progressed, which is how the Longhorns obliterated very good offenses in Kansas and TCU later in the season.

If Texas had been better on money downs, the Horns would have been unquestionably the league's best defense. Fill in the season record for yourself if Texas had held opponents to a 30-33% conversion rate, but your guess should be double digit wins.

Poor Baylor couldn't get off of the field on money downs. Part of the reason Dave Aranda fired his defensive coordinator.

What about advanced statistics, which factor in opponent strength, meaningful turnover creation (a pick six in a contested game is a lot more meaningful than intercepting an end of half garbage time hail mary), minimizes garbage time impact and generally attempts to contextualize the data?

FEI NATIONAL RANK

Team	Rank
Iowa State	7
Kansas State	9
Texas	10
TCU	24
Texas Tech	27
Oklahoma State	30
Oklahoma	43
Baylor	48
West Virginia	100
Kansas	107

Advanced statistics are a major improvement over gross statistics, but they are not the final word as they don't factor in key injuries, weather, game context. Similarly, the idea that pure metrics can differentiate the challenge level of Alabama as opposed to UMass can be fallacious, even if they have statistical controls that purport to tease that out.

Interesting aside: while all fans rightfully love sacking the quarterback, Texas Tech led the league in sacks and still surrendered 6.2 yards per play. Meanwhile, Iowa State was dead last in QB sacks and led the league in most team defense categories. .

So what matters most in evaluating modern defense?

FOUR THINGS:

1. Getting off of the field on 3rd and 4th down.

2. Yards per play allowed.

3. Red zone defense.

4. Mayhem. Meaning: turnover creation and non-offensive scoring.

It's hard for traditionalists to see scoring defense absent above, as it used to be the only metric that defined defense, but scoring defense is a result of those distinct categories (in combination with the offense and special teams taking care of the ball), not a trait in and of itself. The four listed parameters can actually be practiced, coached, recruited to, and analyzed individually. Scoring defense is a byproduct of those things.

What does this mean for Texas in 2023? Texas is nearly guaranteed to play good defense. There's too much returning talent and experience not to excel in their third year in the system. If the Horns show considerable improvement in getting off of the field on money downs and mayhem creation, they will be an elite unit. It starts up front.

DEFENSIVE LINE|EDGE

Player	Height	Weight	Class
T'Vondre Sweat	6'4"	355	SR
Alfred Collins	6'5"	313	SR
Barryn Sorrell	6'3"	262	JR
Byron Murphy II	6'1"	300	JR
Vernon Broughton	6'4"	300	JR
Justice Finkley	6'2"	250	SO
Ethan Burke	6'6"	250	SO
Aaron Bryant	6'2"	300	FR/RS
Jaray Bledsoe	6'4"	266	FR/RS
D.J. Harris	6'2"	235	FR/RS
Zac Swanson	6'4"	259	FR/RS
Kristopher Ross	6'2"	246	FR/RS
J'mond Tapp	6'3"	261	FR/RS
Colton Vasek	6'5"	230	FR
Sydir Mitchell	6'6"	359	FR
Billy Walton	6'2"	215	FR

Tackles

	Solo	Ast	TFL	Sack	Total	PBU	QBH	FF	FR
Barryn Sorrell	16	28	9	5.5	44	1	7	1	
T'Vondre Sweat	10	20	2.5		30	4	7		
Byron Murphy II	9	17	3	1	26		2		
Alfred Collins	7	10	3	1	17		3		
Justice Finkley	1	6	.5	.5	7		1		
Vernon Broughton	5	2	1		7		4		
Ethan Burke	5	1	1.5		6		1		
Kristopher Ross		2			2				
J'Mond Tapp	0	1			1		1		

Byron Murphy is a powerful asset on the Longhorn interior defensive line and the former 3 star recruit plays with a chip on his shoulder and a fire in his belly. The compact Murphy is excellent at submarining taller offensive linemen and he is one of the strongest Longhorns in the weight room. Don't credit Texas for that. He showed up that way. Last year, the presence of Moro Ojomo and Keondre Coburn cut into his snaps, but now Murphy is an indispensable team leader who will have the lead role in an impressive defensive tackle rotation. Murphy now has 25 games under his belt and given the confluence between his ability, experience and opportunity, he should have a very good year. Byron is a tough-minded leader and is an enforcer on the field and in the locker room. His get off has always been a plus, but in the Spring game it looked elite as he tipped a ball and earned a sack when the coaches let him hunt.

T'Vondre Sweat needs a strong final season to ensure his NFL draft status and the quality of his play will determine whether his name is called on Day 2 or Day 3. Sweat was once a svelte 240 pound high school defensive end at Huntsville, but after adding approximately one Tri Delt to his body weight, he mans the middle for the Texas defense. Sweat has played a lot of football at Texas – appearing in 48 games - and the veteran is poised for his most impactful season to date. In 2022, he had a career high 30 tackles to go with 7 quarterback hurries and 4 batted balls. He also showed more impact as a pass rusher, altering throws and getting passers to feel his presence. Historically, Sweat has done a fine job of holding the line of scrimmage at nose tackle and he can play 3 technique when the Horns want to bully a weak guard, but his NFL potential will only be realized if he plays his final season on the 40 Acres like a contract year with all of the urgency that entails. Too often Sweat is content with simply doing his job and securing his gap rather than completely wrecking the guy across from him and altering the game. Over his career, Sweat has compiled 9.5 tackles for loss, 3 sacks and 10 batted passes. Statistics for big men can be deceiving, but a contract year motivated Sweat should try to match those numbers this season.

Alfred Collins had a big offseason. Emphasis on big. Collins focused on gaining weight, committing fully to the notion that he is an inside player in his fourth and likely final year in Austin. Consequently, #95 now rolls around at 6-5, 310 without a hint of sloppiness and has the size and strength to handle double teams. Play strength has improved commensurately while athletic burst is undiminished. Collins is arguably the best pure talent on the Longhorn defensive line, but he has never fully put it together. There's plenty of blame to go around on that front, but Collins looks terrific going into his final season. A former basketball standout, Collins has unusual coordination and movement for an athlete of his size and he is now doing a better job of maintaining low pads, shedding blocks, hand placement, and understanding how blockers are attacking him. Collins can play disruptive 3 technique (outside shoulder of the guard), but he has the athletic ability to be employed throughout Pete Kwiatkoswki's preferred fronts. For his career, Collins has 10.5 tackles for loss and 4.5 sacks and he may just match those numbers in his final season.

Trill Carter joins a stocked defensive tackle room to make it the league's deepest and most formidable from top to bottom. The 4th year transfer from Minnesota started 24 games in

Minneapolis and was Honorable Mention All Big 10 in 2022. Over three years of game action, Carter has 55 tackles, 4 sacks and 8.5 tackles for loss playing both nose tackle and defensive end in a 3 man front. Carter is versatile, plays with high effort and doesn't mind doing the dirty work. Though optimistically listed at 6-2, he's probably closer to 6'0. Carter is likely the 4th best option of the Longhorn interior defensive linemen, but given that he was a two year starter on a quality Gopher defense, that should give you some idea as to the talent around him. Carter would certainly start at most other Big 12 schools. Expect him to play 25-30 hard snaps per game and return for a larger role in 2024.

Sydir Mitchell looks every bit of 6-6, 360 and the true freshman inhabits multiple zip codes on the defensive line. Sydir is carrying a lot of bad weight, which makes his play on the field all the more impressive. He's an absolute problem for offenses when he's fresh, standing up run blockers like they hit a brick wall and effectively collapsing pockets on passing downs like a bear jumping on a tent. He needs to remake his body and that won't be hard to do if he's committed to it. Despite the quality ahead of him, Texas will play him this year. He has too much potential and they need to get him ready for 2024. Just make sure he doesn't get caught on the field when a team goes hurry up. Sydir Mitchell is an NFL player if he wants to be one.

Vernon Broughton is a 4th year junior who will have to fight hard for his snaps this year. Broughton has explosiveness out of his stance and is capable of a good initial strike on blockers, particularly as a pass rusher, but high pads and an inability to gain leverage prevent him from having more impact on the field. Until he gets stronger and plays lower, Broughton will continue to see his snaps diminish.

Aaron Bryant is a redshirt freshman from Mississippi who has seen limited action in his young Longhorn career. Given the talent ahead of him, that's no knock on Bryant. He won't have a ton of opportunities for reps this year, so spending some extra time in the weight room and practice field could set him up nicely for a wide open competition in 2024.

Jaray Bledsoe is a redshirt freshman with raw ability, but he is currently caught in the no-man's land of body composition between playing edge and defensive tackle. Alfred Collins might have a few words for him about the importance of committing to the body weight where you project, but Bledsoe still has some time to see where his body and the staff want to take him.

Spring revealed that **Zac Swanson** is an undersized but game pass rusher from the interior. Good first step, uses his hands well and gets small going through gaps so that guards struggle to get a good piece of him. #86 could actually be a nice depth addition to be employed against passing offenses in this role. He can't handle normal down run responsibilities inside, but using him to spell Longhorn pass rushers against prolific spread teams makes sense. Naturally, one must wonder if he can play edge, but his athletic traits don't appear to translate that way.

Barryn Sorrell has blossomed nicely in his time at Texas. The 6-4, 260 pound power rusher from New Orleans sets the edge well and does a fine job extending his arms and working through or around blockers. Hustle is always present and Sorrell doesn't take plays off.

He has improved against the run since his true freshman debut and his play against the run game this season should be a strength. He is coming off a 44 tackle, 5.5 sack, 9 tackle for loss and 7 quarterback hurries performance in 2022. Those are very productive numbers, but Texas needs even more from its best edge if the Longhorn defense is going to be elite. Sorrell has improved every year since he has been in Austin and there is no reason to think that his junior season won't be even better than last year. There is no more valuable asset on the Longhorn defense other than Jaylan Ford given the options behind him.

Ethan Burke is a true sophomore from Austin Westlake who made a nice leap this Spring to battle for the starting edge job opposite Barryn Sorrell. Burke is very tall and has re-shaped his body, but still a bit light for his frame. Burke uses his wingspan well and will do it even better once he is 270 pounds. Right now, he's not strong enough at the point of attack and he needs an interior flush or stunts to get to the quarterback consistently. The former all-state lacrosse player is very mobile and his combination of length and change of direction makes him a potentially dangerous pass rusher, but he's still physically unde-veloped. Burke played a little in 2022 and this summer will be crucial for him to add weight and strength so that he can bring more juice to his skill set.

Justice Finkley impressed with his maturity, focus and developed body as a true freshman, but he is a compact 250 pound edge trying to win with motor and strength rather than elite speed or change of direction. That's a tall order for a short edge. Finkley will outwork less gifted offensive tackles and he's good on the move when he can attack interior gaps on a stunt, but smaller edges better have outstanding quickness and power to make up for their lack of length if they want to be effective pass rushers. So far, that has not been Finkley. Justice is a capable player with a great work ethic and a motor, but unless he can add more suddenness or pass rushing moves to his repertoire, the sophomore's ceiling may already be topping out.

J'Mond Tapp looks the part, but the redshirt freshman from Louisiana had a poor Spring game going against the Longhorn starters and made a few plays on blown assignments against walk-ons and true freshmen. Tapp has the frame and athletic ability, so check back in late August to see if he's playing with more abandon and violence.

Kris Ross lost about twenty five pounds to try out the edge position and with that weight loss, he also lost some play strength. He has a good first step, but has shown little power through contact and is too easily stalemated. His offseason should be focused on getting stronger if he wants to be a viable edge.

Billy Walton and **Colton Vasek** are all exciting young additions, but it's not clear whether the true freshmen will play much yet.

Prognosis

Texas may have the deepest group of defensive tackles in the country. The top four in the rotation – Murphy, Collins, Sweat, Carter – will be empowered to go full speed every down knowing that they will not have to play heavy snaps and their quality and depth may give Pete Kwiatkoswki the latitude to play three big interior guys at a time to compensate for the lack of proven edges. As part of a larger 3-2-6 defense, it might be an extremely productive wrinkle for pass-oriented teams or any team without the physicality to punish a light box.

Overall, Big 12 running offenses will struggle to do much between the tackles against the Longhorn base defense, particularly given that the other vertex of the interior triangle is Jaylan Ford. Throw in the need to get undeniable talent Sydir Mitchell a few snaps and there will be plenty of mayhem to go around. The main struggle Bo Davis will face is convincing Bledsoe, Bryant, Swanson and Broughton to bide their time and stick around as plenty of snaps open up in 2024.

Texas has a rock solid edge in Barryn Sorrell, but the other starting edge will be the weak link on a 4 man front. That is a relative statement. As long as that player is at least average, Texas will still have a very good front. Right now, Ethan Burke will battle Justice Finley for that role while the staff tries out different alignments and personnel groups to find the best fit. The edge solution on some downs may be freshman linebacker Anthony Hill, particularly if Burke and Finkley can't show a pass rush against higher end offensive tackles.

Last year, Texas led the country in pressures but finished with only 20 sacks. Much of that is on the Longhorn secondary needing to challenge receivers more on key downs so the rush can get home, but a good bit of it is also on Texas defensive linemen finishing plays and constricting the pocket with better containment. Getting quarterbacks on the ground a half dozen times more might have been the difference between 12-2 and 8-5 last year.

LINEBACKER

Player	Height	Weight	Class
Jaylan Ford	6'3"	236	SR
David Gbenda	6'0"	231	SR
Jett Bush	6'2"	245	SR
Morice Blackwell, Jr.	6'1"	213	JR
Anthony Hill Jr.	6'3"	229	FR
Liona Lefau	6'1"	227	FR
Derion Gullette	6'3"	234	FR
Tausili Akana	6'3"	195	FR
S'Maje Burrell	6'0"	215	FR

Tackles										
	Solo	Ast	TFL	Sack	Total	PBU	QBH	INT	FF	FR
Jaylan Ford	61	58	10	2	119	2	2	4	3	2
Jett Bush	10	7			17					
David Gbenda		8	4		12					
Morice Blackwell Jr.		7	4	1	5					

Jaylan Ford was a wonderful surprise last year after emerging as the most productive linebacker on the team over the back half of 2021. The quantum leap he made from 2021 to 2022 was reflected in his postseason honors. The Longhorn Defensive MVP and 1st Team All Big 12 standout was a productivity machine, totaling 119 tackles, 10 tackles for loss, 2 sacks, 4 interceptions, 3 forced fumbles and 2 recovered fumbles. Ford was effectively responsible for 7 of the 14 turnovers that the defense created all season. Props to Ford and shame on the other ten starters. The heart of the Longhorn defense evolved into a fantastic pass defender and a classic off-the-ball run stopper who was as capable of making the fundamental play as the spectacular one. Though Ford lacks elite speed or quickness, he has elite intangible football traits and exhibits a strong nose for the ball. Ford is a sound tackler with a high football IQ and given the trajectory of his growth from sophomore to junior, it's a good bet that his senior season will be special. Ford is the most important

player on the Texas defense and despite some very good talent around him, #2 isn't very close.

David Gbenda is an undersized 5th year junior linebacker who has appeared in 32 contests. The squatty but quick Gbenda fits the mold of the spread-busting linebacker archetype that proliferates in the Big 12, but Texas fans are still waiting for Gbenda to put it together and become a more instinctive player. Far too frequently, David gets caught chasing ghosts, putting him out of position and allowing offenses to run or throw the ball to his vacant space. Continuity in the system and more time in a defined role should help him. Gbenda's positive attributes are that he has been a sure tackler when he makes the right read and he doesn't mind contact. Whether officially a starter or not, Gbenda is going to play 400-500+ snaps this year.

Anthony Hill, not Arch Manning, was the talk of the offseason for thinking fans. Hill had a great deal of buzz around him throughout spring practice and the offseason, but the Spring game was his public debut. It did not disappoint. The 230 pound Hill showed elite quickness and is already the best blitzer and pure edge pass rusher on the team. He's cheetah quick, refuses blocking, with motor and recovery in spades. He's not just a finesse guy either. On one play where he couldn't find a gap to shimmy through and the ball was already out, he chose to detonate 360 pound Payton Kirkland just because he could. Hill chose violence. Any linebacker who decides to blow someone up because he can is a linebacker we want on the field.

Can Hill reliably play the run as a traditional linebacker? Probably not yet, but we'll see. That's fine given that Texas has plenty of built-in run-stopping at several other positions. Texas needs Hill's explosiveness and pass rush ability. Hill's depth chart position may say linebacker, but if Texas is smart, he will be a disruptor who lines up all over the field and attacks the quarterback like a wolverine on bacon. From that perspective, Hill can play every linebacker position because he'll still be blitzing wherever he's lined up. While Hill can provide an edge rush, he is not big enough to hold up there as an every down solution.

Jett Bush is back for a second year at his natural position at off-the-ball linebacker after a 2021 detour playing edge where he racked up 14 tackles, 3.5 tackles for loss, and a single sack. The former walk-on lacked ideal size and length for edge play, but roster desperation and Bush's willingness to give up his body in the running game earned him a fair number of snaps. He shifted back to linebacker last year. In his senior season, he looks to be ready for a strong final campaign. In the Spring game, Bush was the second best linebacker against the run behind Jaylan Ford and he looked very comfortable in the scheme overall. The 245 pound Bush has solid range, certainly much better than the average fan's perception of him. He led the team in tackles in the 1st half of the scrimmage and he made a variety of good plays, to include a terrific goal line stop on Blue, a nice read on a screen, along with a sack on Arch coming off of the edge on a stunt. He will play quite a bit in 2023 as a key reserve.

Morice Blackwell is built like a safety but hits like a linebacker. The fact that he runs like a linebacker is why he doesn't play safety. He is comfortable in space and embraces contact, but the 210 pound athlete is smaller than some members of the wide receiver room and he doesn't have elite speed to compensate for his size deficit. He does have plenty of attitude and bad intentions though. The hard-hitting junior will certainly see playing time in a paper thin linebacker room, but coaches will probably slant his snaps towards certain offenses.

Liona Lefau, **Tausili Akana**, **S'Maje Burrell**, **Derion Gullette** (injury) are all true freshmen who represent vital depth. Lefau has the best chance to play early and the staff love his football intelligence.

Prognosis

The steady and prolific Jaylan Ford is the centerpiece of the linebacking corps and freshman Anthony Hill represents terrific upside as a general instrument of destruction. Those two represent the ceiling for this defense. The floor of the unit will be decided by the potential for steady play from David Gbenda, Jett Bush, Morice Blackwell and freshman Liona Lefau. If they can contribute quality snaps and play reliably while spelling or complementing the upside guys, the Longhorns will have a strong tie-in between a strong secondary and a good defensive line. Spelling Ford and not overloading the young phenom Hill is crucial over a long season. The gap between Texas' best linebackers and their backups is the most pronounced on the team and it's imperative that the offseason and some early non-con games are utilized to build depth and narrow that gap.

DEFENSIVE BACK

Player	Height	Weight	Class
Kitan Crawford	5'11"	201	SR
Jahdae Barron	5'11"	191	SR
Ryan Watts	6'3"	206	SR
Jerrin Thompson	6'0"	190	SR
Jalen Catalon	5'10"	194	SR
Gavin Holmes	5'11"	168	JR
Terrance Brooks	6'0"	200	SO
Jaylon Guilbeau	6'0"	178	SO
Austin Jordan	6'0"	202	SO
Michael Taaffe	6'0"	189	SO
Larry Turner-Gooden	6'0"	199	FR/RS
B.J. Allen Jr.	6'1"	207	FR/RS
X'avion Brice	6'1"	177	FR/RS
Malik Muhammad	6'0"	177	FR
Jelani McDonald	6'2"	200	FR
Derek Williams	6'2"	200	FR
Warren Roberson	6'0"	190	FR

	Solo	Ast	TFL	Total	PBU	INT	QBH	FF	FR
Jerrin Thompson	50	33	.5	83	7	1			
Jahdae Barron	43	35	11.5	78	3	2	1		1
Ryan Watts	33	18	4	51	3	1	1		
Michael Taaffe	13	13	.5	26	1				
Kitan Crawford	17	8		25	2				
Jaylon Guilbeau	8	11		19	2		4		
Terrance Brooks	5	4	.5	9	3				
Austin Jordan	4	3	.5	7					

Jahdae Barron wasn't a starter to begin the year, but he quickly seized the nickel role as his speed, quickness and anticipation were impossible to keep off of the field. In 9 starts and 13 games, Barron was the 4th leading tackler on the team with 78 stops, two interceptions and scooped and scored a fumble for a touchdown against TCU. Barron also led the defense in tackles for loss. That's atypical for a nickelback, but Barron's ability to recognize and blow up the screen game and aspects of the outside run game is so profound that he notched 11.5 tackles behind the line of scrimmage.

The senior from Pflugerville Connally is probably the most underrated defender in the Big 12 and his ability to control the slot receiver 1-on-1 and his pure coverage tenacity gives Texas coverage versatility and was a reason for the improvement in the Longhorn defense from 2021 to 2022. Barron is also very good against the run despite average size, largely owed to his decisiveness, quickness and aggression. Jahdae can also play cornerback and the coaches will keep that skillset in their pocket if ever needed. Right now, his greatest contribution to the team is at nickel. Barron is an outstanding player and one of the three most important players on the defense.

Ryan Watts had a strong debut in Austin after transferring in from Ohio State. The 6-3, 205 pound corner is a good tackler and reliable coverage asset who totaled 51 tackles,

1 interception and a sack. Watts is physical in coverage and relishes coming up in run support, offering the Horns the flexibility of playing extra defensive backs without losing physicality and tackling. Watts does not possess great speed, but if he can do his work early rerouting receivers and changing the timing of the offense, he flourishes.

Throughout his career, there has been some thought of playing Watts at safety to take advantage of his tackling and lateral range, but that move will only be considered if another cornerback can play at a high level in his stead. That's unlikely in his senior year and he is the odds on favorite to be the starter at cornerback. He's just too big, sound, aggressive and athletic to keep him off of the field, even if some feel other corners in the program may be better in pure man-coverage.

Gavin Holmes comes to Austin from Wake Forest and Texas coaches are hoping that the speedy cornerback will play as well as fellow transfer Ryan Watts did last year. Holmes is unlikely to be confused with Watts anytime soon – he is four inches shorter and nearly forty pounds lighter. However, don't get too caught up in size as it's important to see the Wake Forest for the trees. Holmes is a cat quick man coverage specialist with a change of direction that any cornerback would envy; gazelle-footed with good lateral quickness and excellent mirroring ability. The junior from New Orleans played a great deal at Wake, starting 14 games but appearing in 28 total. Longhorn coaches were impressed by his quickness and he's a good bet to start in what should be a lively cornerback competition that lasts all season. Holmes is slightly built so concerns about his physicality, his ability to compete with and win balls against much bigger receivers and how he will hold up in the run game won't be fully addressed until the pads start popping.

Terrance Brooks improved considerably over the course of the season, earning three starts and nine game appearances as a true freshman. Brooks blew some coverages last year, but also drew favorable attention in his first start of the season against a high level TCU wide receiver corps, notching four solo tackles and more than holding his own. He really turned heads playing in the Alamo Bowl against Washington's elite QB and wide receivers, notching two pass breakups and playing a big part in holding Michael Penix to one of his statistically worst performances of the season. If Gavin Holmes is a gazelle at cornerback, the 6-0, 200 pound Brooks is all horsepower: big, powerful, straight line fast. He doesn't match the route, he directs the route. At minimum, Brooks is the 3rd cornerback this season and will see extensive snaps; a starter in all but name. At maximum, he's a starter who allows Texas to play much more press man coverage on key downs and will be all over 2025 NFL draft boards.

Jerrin Thompson has started twenty games in his Longhorn career amassing 138 tackles, 2 interceptions and 13 pass breakups. Thompson is not a big safety, but he embraces collisions and he has a good football IQ. The senior will be asked to lead the defense, make the calls in the secondary and provide cover over the top for a talented group of corners and nickelbacks. While tThompson does not possess any one particularly outstanding physical

attribute, he is heady, possesses solid lateral range and he is fearless in run support. He capped off last season with one of his best performances of the year against Washington with 11 tackles (7 solo) and an interception. Texas will need his leadership and reliable play if the defense is going to be a potential Top 10 national unit overall.

Jalen Catalon is a safety with terrific upside and proven abilities at the highest levels of football, but his injury history is worrisome. Catalon played only one game in 2022 before a season-ending shoulder injury. He missed another eight games in 2021 with the same injury while also playing with a broken hand. Before those two injury-stricken seasons and multiple reconstructive surgeries, Catalon was a 1st team All SEC safety who balled out in 2020 with 99 tackles, 2 forced fumbles and 3 interceptions. Catalon was bubble wrapped this offseason as they tried to rehab his body. The Longhorns will treat him as a lottery ticket. If he can play like the old Catalon, the secondary will be that much better. If he can't, Texas coaches will have been smart enough to split up his practice time with the 1s and 2s so that other Texas safeties can take over his role seamlessly. The Texas native is an outstanding teammate and a healthy year from him would be a boon to the program. Unfortunately, the odds may not be in his favor.

Kitan Crawford has the athleticism and physicality that coaches love. He is also one of the best pure athletes on the team. The fourth year senior defensive back has spent most of his Longhorn career at cornerback, but he was moved to safety last year in an attempt to create more playmaking and dynamism there. Crawford did not start, but played extensive snaps in every game, securing a career high 25 tackles. Kitan has an extensive offensive background from high school and demonstrates better than average ball skills and hands. He also has the requisite physicality, runs well, and likes to hit, so what is not to love? The answer is found in the name of his position: safety. A safety who isn't safe on his assignments creates danger for the whole defense. Crawford's learning curve will determine whether he is a 2023 starter. #21 has a lot of desirable traits that the coaches want out on the field, but they won't trade them for the mental mistakes that create busted coverages and open receivers.

Jaylon Guilbeau impressed enough as a true freshman to start the first three games of the season before losing his job to Jahdae Barron and then missing the last fives games of the season with a knee injury. His rehab continued through the spring, but he should be ready to go in the Fall. In limited action last year, Jaylon totaled 19 tackles, 4 pass break ups and a couple of QB hurries as a blitzer. Guilbeau is very physical and competitive, but he is more quick than fast and should serve as Jahdae Barron's backup at nickel.

Michael Taaffe is a third year sophomore former walk-on from Westlake who will certainly be in the rotation at safety. Now a scholarship player, Taaffe had 26 tackles last year and proved an effective coverage man who doesn't make many mistakes. Taaffe had a good spring game where he tackled well and he should gain even more confidence as he fills out and matures this offseason. Taaffe played extensive snaps against Kansas State last year and did a solid job in run support against a physical offense, notching six tackles (four solo).

BJ Allen was a highly touted high school recruit who is starting to come into his own as a redshirt freshman. The Allen product has filled out since arriving in Austin and will certainly be a special teams player who could press for time at safety. The light is turning on for Allen and that's terrific news for the Longhorn secondary.

X'avion Brice is a wiry, long cornerback from Arlington Seguin who will fight to involve himself in the cornerback rotation.

Austin Jordan played extensively on special teams last year and the sophomore cornerback can also play nickel and safety.

Larry Turner-Gooden is in a crowded room and lacks the speed to make a push for playing time at safety.

Malik Muhammad is a promising young cornerback from DeSoto who is already making his case for snaps in 2023. He will contend for a starting role in 2024.

Jelani McDonald is a very talented all-around athlete who moves with great agility at 6-2, 205. He will start off at nickel, but safety or linebacker could be in his future.

Derek Williams hasn't disappointed since arriving on campus. The highly ranked recruit from Louisiana is still growing and evolving into a future 6-2, 210 pound safety with ball skills. Expect the coaches to get him involved early, despite a crowded secondary.

Warren Roberson has impressed as one of the most explosive freshmen. He will find early work on special teams. His future is bright.

Prognosis

Over the last two years, the Longhorn coaching staff has done an outstanding job upgrading this unit through the portal (Watts, Holmes, Catalon), signing back-to-back outstanding recruiting classes and developing inherited talent. Departing starters Anthony Cook and D'shawn Jamison gave their all for the Horns, but both positions will be upgraded.

Cornerback and nickel now go three deep in quality and there will be intense competition for starting jobs and rotation slots all year. Depth at cornerback is increasingly vital in college football and Texas has it in spades. Safety has an interesting group of options built around senior leader Jerrin Thompson. Those options are contingent on the development of Kitan Crawford, the health of Jalen Catalon, the known quantity of Michael Taaffe, the emergence of BJ Allen and the potential precociousness of outstanding incoming freshman Derek Williams.

The secondary will be better. The question is: how much better?

Last year, the Longhorn pass defense gave up 6.3 yards per passing attempt and only 18 passing touchdowns in over 500 attempts. Opposing receivers averaged only 10 yards per completion. Bryce Young, Michael Penix and Max Duggan had some of their statistically worst passing games of the season against Texas. Tackling was much improved overall and the Longhorn secondary developed a good reputation in run support, particularly returnees Ryan Watts, Jahdae Barron and Jerrin Thompson. This was an improved unit by every metric and the eye test agreed.

Except that they just didn't make enough plays. This was a pass defense that was good at limiting offenses, not dominating them at key moments. In 2023, the main mission for the Longhorn secondary is to exert more control over offenses. In 2022, they forced only 6 interceptions and collectively forced only one fumble. A unit of five defensive backs forcing only 7 turnovers over 13 games is a simple lack of playmaking. If Texas wants to play elite defense instead of pretty good defense, they will need to walk up on receivers on money downs, take more risks, attack more routes and strip more ball carriers. Some of that will be a result of coaching, scheme and emphasis. Much of it will come from playing new faces who are capable of doing those things.

SPECIAL TEAMS

Player	Height	Weight	Class
Will Stone	6'0"	191	JR
Bert Auburn	6'0"	181	SR
Ryan Sandborn	6'3"	195	SR

Bert Auburn returns with the easy confidence of a white man sporting an afro. Sideshow Bert kicked extremely well for Texas last year, connecting on 21 of 26 attempts, including an outstanding 7 of 9 on kicks between 40-49 yards with only one blocked kick attempt. His 80.8% accuracy was good for 4th in Longhorn history. The junior's return is a nice plus for this team and it would only be fitting if a man named Auburn kicks the game-winner in Tuscaloosa. Longhorn opponents were 16 of 21 on their field goal attempts, which was an irritating level of efficiency.

Will Stone handled kickoffs capably and should be improved in his second year handling those duties. He had only 26 touchbacks in 86 attempts and he kicked three balls out of bounds. In fairness, he has exhibited good hang time and placement for his coverage unit.

Punting will be improved. Danny "Machete" Trejo did his best pressed into action, but his lack of hang time and directional control belied a 42 yard average. By advanced metrics, he ranked in the bottom quartile of FBS punters and 2nd from last in the Big 12. Former Stanford punter **Ryan Sanborn** – a four year starter – will replace him. Sanborn doesn't bring an elite leg, but he was the only punter in FBS to go 20 for 20 on attempts to pin opponents inside their 20 yard line and not a single one of his 50 punting attempts went for a touchback. Sanford is gifted at directional placement. He and Trejo will have roughly the same per kick average, but the result in opponent field position and return success should be different.

Longhorn coverage teams were solid overall and in combination with Auburn's reliable kicking, Texas ranked 11th in overall FEI nationally. That number can be matched or exceeded if the Horns can find more kick coverage demons to replace players like Roschon Johnson. Given the increase in athleticism and team speed over the last two recruiting classes, the raw material is there. They just need to find the players with sufficient want-to and aggression.

Longhorn punt returns were negligible, though they did get a block and touchdown by Keilan Robinson. Texas kickoff returns significantly outperformed their opponents. Keilan Robinson averaged a healthy 25.2 yards per return with a season long of 52 yards while Texas opponents collectively averaged only 17.2 yards per return with a season long of only 34 yards.

Most of the key components of the Texas special teams are back or have been improved. If Jeff Banks can identify a couple of coverage maniacs and get more out of the punt block and return game, this projects to be a Top 10 national unit.

RICE OWLS

September 2 | Austin, TX

2022 RECORD	POINTS SCORED	POINTS ALLOWED
5-8	25.2	34.2
Not Ranked	#84 of 131	#121 of 131

CONFERENCE USA

Mike Bloomgren | 6th season
2022 conference record 3-5

RETURNING STARTERS

OFFENSE - 4 | DEFENSE - 5

Overview

Rice is a Bayou Ivy dedicated to the pursuit of knowledge and rational inquiry featuring a school band of irreverent virgins that plays polkas on kazoos with the playful acronym of The M.O.B. Rice itself is an acronym for Rest Ice Compression Elevation, which has generally been the recommended postgame treatment for the Owls after facing Texas.

Decades ago, John F Kennedy challenged Americans to seek challenge and adventure, asking rhetorically,"Why does Rice play Texas?" There is a practical answer to that. Rice gets to pick up a check and Texas gets a win. The Owls have lost fifteen in a row to the Longhorns, but all Longhorn fans of a certain generation remember the Rice upset in 1994, a humiliating 19-17 loss on a Sunday night in Houston played in monsoonal conditions. Texas suspended four starters before the game for a curfew violation (including star receivers Mike Adams and Lovell Pinkney) and the Owls had a couple of NFL players in their front 7. If you just had a brief flashback of N.D. Kalu sacking Shea Morenz on a twelve step drop back in sideways rain, I share your trauma. That evening Texas coach John Mackovic taught Longhorn players the importance of discipline and he taught Texas fans the importance of establishing the pass during a typhoon without starting receivers.

Before that regrettable little incident, the Owls hadn't beaten Texas since 1965.

So you're saying there's a chance?

Well, probably not.

Rice will bring back most of its starters and added a couple of interesting portal transfers from a 5-8 team that lost in the Lending Tree Bowl Game. Yes, we live in a world where 5-7 teams go to bowl games. Leave it to Lending Tree to extend a losing team easy credit. Nonetheless, 2022 was the best Owl squad in head coach Mike Bloomgren's 5 year tenure (he's 16-39 over than span) and while that's damning with faint praise, this team looks to be even better. If they can catch a few breaks and their passing game dominates their peers, the Owls have a very good shot at going to another bowl game.

Originally, Bloomgren tried to transplant the physical, pro-style approach that he won with as the offensive coordinator at Stanford to Rice and counting on physically dominating the other team isn't the best plan of action for Rice's athletic profile. Particularly in a state where spread athletes are found in abundance. They have wisely expanded their plan of attack from repetitively running inside zone to throwing the ball around and relying on skill, brains and quickness over brawn. The Owls will have an outside shot at beating a Big 12 opponent in September, but that team won't wear Burnt Orange. That Big 12 opponent is ten minutes from their campus and wears scarlet and white.

Crickets chirping.

I'm talking about Houston. Houston is in the Big 12 now, guys. Keep up.

Strengths

Rice is badly outmatched across the board, but when Texas plays a lesser early season opponent, it's important to isolate one or two of the opponent's strengths at the unit or position level and see how they match up against the Longhorn unit tasked with facing them.

The unit test(s) of interest will be the Owl passing game – specifically the Owl receivers and new quarterback – against the Longhorn pass defense. The Owls will be led by JT Daniels now playing for his 4th university. Don't let the dream die, Wooderson! Count his schools with me: USC, Georgia, West Virginia, Rice. His school progression has been the human embodiment of water finding its level. Next stop, Wellesley. Despite college eligibility that began during the Suez Crisis, Daniels has never lived fully up to his high school pedigree, but he has started 29 FBS football games and he has a live arm. Amassing 6947 passing yards, 45 touchdowns and 25 interceptions over six years as an itinerant laborer is no easy task. Daniels is a ramblin' man who carries his earthly possessions in a kerchief tied to a stick and if you leave a pie cooling in a window near a rail line, he may just help himself. He's now lost starting jobs at three different stops.

Daniels can spin the ball but he lacks feel and mobility (is negative 295 career rushing yards good?) and he doesn't always see the field well when coverages are more opaque. Seeing the field is a useful quality in a position tasked with looking for guys in the same colored jersey who are receiver eligible, but if he gets predictable coverages and a clean pocket, one quickly understands why he will probably stick around the NFL as a journeyman back up. His arrival meant the departure of former starting QB TJ McMahon to Marshall and while Daniels is inarguably a tangbile upgrade, intangibles haven't always been his forte.

The real standout unit for the Owls is the receiving corps. Team MVP Bradley Rozner was fantastic in 2022, leading the Owls with 44 catches for 876 yards and 10 touchdowns on a nearly 20 yard per catch average. Rozner is a true X receiver and he wins balls with a 6-5, 205 pound frame, wingspan and long stride athleticism. He had at least one touchdown and 100+ yards in 8 of his 12 starts. He is capable of a one strike big play score, even against Texas. Disrupting his route early is crucial.

He's complemented by 6-2, 200 pound Luke McCaffrey, younger brother of NFL star RB Christian, son of former John Elway target Ed McCaffrey. Luke caught 58 balls for 723 yards last year and while he has solid speed, his greatest gift is quickness and he's most comfortable operating in the short and midrange game. He'll run at least one reverse a game and the former QB is a threat to throw. The third member of the trio is Cedric Patterson. Patterson missed most of 2022, but was a primary target in 2021, amassing 581 yards and 6 touchdowns. They also have a quality tight end in 6-5, 255 pound Jack Bradley.

In aggregate, this unit would be a middle tier Big 12 receiving corps and Daniels is certainly an above average pure passer, albeit with some significant flaws. The Texas pass defense will get a needed early test, even if the Longhorns gobble up Rice everywhere else.

Weaknesses

The Owl offensive line returns four starters and adds a former Nebraska backup OL, but they're more experienced than good. The Owl running game should also be unremarkable. They will be just fine in their games against Texas Southern, Florida Atlantic and Charlotte (the school, not just some random girl; she wouldn't stand a chance) but facing Byron Murphy, Alfred Collins, Jaylan Ford and Barryn Sorrell will be a different animal entirely. Rice needs to get the ball out quickly given JT Daniels' inability to run or navigate a collapsing pocket and if Texas has confidence in their defensive backs playing tight coverage, interception opportunities will abound. Rice will take their deep shots from max protection and Texas defensive backs need to understand formation and game context so they don't get caught napping.

Defensively, Rice surrendered 6.5 yards per play and 34.1 points per game last year. Opponents averaged a sizzling 5.4 yards per carry and a healthy 7.9 yards per passing attempt. This may be a good opportunity to get the Longhorn run game on track once Ewers and company soften them up in the air. From an efficiency perspective, Football Outsiders ranked the Owls 113th in team defense and that's not going to cut it against quality offenses.. Rice has some quickness at linebacker and at edge, but they struggle to anchor at the line of scrimmage and the secondary can't credibly play man coverage against higher end receivers for four quarters. If Texas executes, they should carb load on the Rice defense in preparation for Alabama while keeping their best playbook wrinkles concealed. If Texas does show some razzle-dazzle, it's a throwaway simply to put on film and make Alabama waste prep time on a play they won't see in Tuscaloosa.

ALABAMA CRIMSON TIDE

September 9 | Tuscaloosa, AL

SOUTHEASTERN CONFERENCE
Nick Saban | 17th season
2022 conference record 6-2

2022 RECORD	POINTS SCORED	POINTS ALLOWED
11-2	41.1	18.2
#5 Final AP Rank	#4 of 131	#9 of 131

RETURNING STARTERS
OFFENSE - 4 | DEFENSE - 5

Overview

You know Nick Saban has built a juggernaut in Tuscaloosa when his 2022 squad that finished 11-2 and ranked 5th in the country was considered disappointing by Tide faithful and led to both coordinators finding alternative employment in the offseason. The overwhelming preseason #1 got the level of exceptional play expected of Bryce Young at quarterback, but the Tide were not as dominant as usual on the lines of scrimmage and their wide receiver corps proved to no longer be the endless 1st round skill factory that they've churned out over the last half decade. Consequently, they lost close games to Tennessee and LSU while barely edging Texas, Texas A&M and Ole Miss. Folks eager to predict the fall of Alabama point to these contests as proof of their shaky footing, but Alabama was much closer to going undefeated as they were to 8-4. They had eight players selected in the 2023 NFL draft and advanced statistics rated them the third best outfit in the country behind Georgia and Ohio State last year. Texas fans would love to have a wobbly season of failure like that.

Saban is responsible for the most dominant college football epoch in the annals of the game. As evidenced by his remarkable 189-27 record and six national titles. Add another title at LSU and you have an unimpeachable argument that Saban is the most accomplished college football coach of all time. At age 71, he is showing no signs of slowing down though enemy recruiters like to point to his advanced years and query recruits whether Saban can really do this much longer. As long as Saban's Just For Men hair dye and his platform cleats hold out, why can't his football mind? He will probably topple over at 100 years old

while running out of the tunnel against Auburn and immediately ascend to football heaven, where he will lecture God on His lack of fundamentals and poor organizational skills.

Saban does not evidence any of the tell-tale characteristics of an old coach who has excelled at the highest levels of the game. Nothing makes you quite so complacent as success, but in Saban one finds little to no self-satisfaction or stubbornness. A masterful program builder, Saban has always evolved with the times as a coach, recruiter, and staff manager, showing remarkable adaptability to cutting edge trends, staff composition and enforced creative destruction, while still maintaining core beliefs centered around toughness, unselfishness and the Bama Machine being bigger than any one player or coach. Saban has little sentimentality for how he thinks the game should be played and adapts both on and off the field to its requirements like a young, hungry innovator rather than a self-satisfied legend.

Saban worships The Process and his zealotry has not diminished. Those who dishonor The Process are "rat poison" who must be expelled from the program whether they be player, coach or any local Alabama media who lack the requisite levels of sycophancy.

One gets the sense that sometimes Saban will just fire a coach, berate a reporter, or lay the wood to a player for no reason other than he senses a whiff of self-congratulation in the air and someone needs to pay for it.

Nick Saban turned over both coordinators this offseason, ditching Bill O' Brien and bringing on Notre Dame offensive coordinator Tommy Rees, while Alabama defensive coordinator Pete Golding migrated to Oxford as veteran Auburn defensive coordinator Kevin Steele rejoined his old nemesis and colleague in Tuscaloosa. Rees was a somewhat controversial hire as Notre Dame's offense wasn't exactly cutting edge (in his defense: Drew Pyne), but Saban wants a renewed emphasis on the running game and play action passing rather than continuing to put the game on the shoulders of the quarterback and receivers in a pass-happy spread. This isn't curmudgeonly regression so much as an honest appraisal of his current roster. Bryce Young is gone. Throwing the ball 45 times a game with a questionable quarterback and a diminished wide receiver corps is foolish.

Defensively, the 64 year old Kevin Steele will bring deep experience and the occasional curveball game plan. Steele believes in pressure, but typically achieves it by bringing unexpected pass rushers rather than jailhouse blitzes. That represents a different mindset from Pete Golding who grew increasingly basic and base-minded over his time in Tuscaloosa. Perhaps Golding worried too much about what the offense was trying to do to the defense rather than what his defense was going to do to the offense. Saban's constant drumbeat in the offseason was for the defense to create more turnovers and for the offense to have fewer – Alabama was an uncharacteristic -2 in turnover margin on the season – and Nick is not one to engage in idle chatter. His hires and rhetoric signal a shift in tactics on both sides of the ball. The Tide are going to be more aggressive on defense and more conservative on offense.

Alabama will be looking to grind down opponents 31-17, not engaging in 45-31 shootouts. Nick Saban is signaling a change towards the run-heavy pace-sensitive Alabama national title teams led by Jacob Coker and AJ McCarron, not the record-setting offenses led by Tua Tagovailoa and Mac Jones. Whether you believe Alabama has taken a step back in talent or not (they have at the sexy skill positions), Saban understands that Bama is hard to beat when they take care of the ball and turn over the opposing offense. As for program talent dropoff or Bama losing their fire on the recruiting trail? The 2023 Tide recruiting class signed seven 5 star recruits and finished ranked 1st in the country. Yeah, this program is wilting and dying, alright.

Strengths

The Alabama defensive line should be improved after a mediocre 2022, featuring a promising mix of established veterans with an infusion of younger dynamic players who should see big jumps in their performance. Redshirt senior Justin Egboigbe (6-5, 290) and senior Tim Smith (6-4, 300) will anchor the front next to big nose tackle Jaheim Oatis (6-5, 330). Smith and Egboigbe are seasoned veterans who do all of the right things while Oatis represents massive upside. Oatis got his weight down enough to start as a freshman and earn All-SEC freshman honors, but he made another leap this offseason and is going to be a major handful at the point of attack. All three interior defensive linemen are backed by quality talent who should provide more disruption as situational pass rushers than what Bama saw from the unit last year. Any offense that can't handle Oatis inside will be behind the eight ball given Alabama's quality on the edge and high level interior linebackers.

Alabama's remarkable 2023 recruiting class won't be asked to contribute at most positions, but keep an eye on freshman safety Caleb Downs and standout running back Justice Haynes. Downs will start as a true freshman at strong safety and given Saban's emphasis on secondary play, that's a compliment to the #1 ranked defensive back in the 2023 class. Downs is an aggressive tackler with elite ball skills. Justice Haynes could have a comparable impact at running back. The five star runner from Buford, GA was a Bulldog football legacy but he chose Tuscaloosa to compete for the starting job against returning runner Jase McClellan, who rushed for 655 yards last year on only 112 carries. Haynes has elite quickness, sweet feet and 360 vision, but ordinary top end speed. Bama will play him early and often and the running back position should be a timeshare as the Tide seek to re-establish their run game bona fides.

Alabama linebacker play took a major loss with the departure of Will Anderson, but even with that fall off, the unit will still remain a plus compared to everyone else in college football. Poor Bama starts two former five star recruits on the edge to help ease the pain of his departure. Texas fans are familiar with Dallas Turner, who knocked Quinn Ewers out of the game in Austin, and Turner is a top 1% athlete at the position who had a little bit of a sophomore slump (his sack total fell from 8.5 to 4.0) after a sensational freshman debut. He will be pinning his ears back more with Kevin Steele calling the shots and he should have a big year. He'll be joined by the bigger and more physical Chris Braswell, who goes 6-3, 255 and is an effective pass rusher, but Braswell will be asked to anchor the run defense and let Steele turn Turner loose more often on neutral downs. Bama's interior backers must replace a departed NFL player, but Bama insiders believe that this is a group that mixes both depth and talent three men deep. Deontae Lawson and Trezmen Marshall should lead an impressive rotation, but some talented youngsters will push for snaps.

Last year, the Tide offensive line was average by their high standards (the Longhorn defensive line largely outplayed them in Austin), but several returning starters have leveled up and intense spring competition led to the elevation of some talented youngsters. The change at coordinator means that Bama is reacquainting itself with low pad levels and power football and the personnel are now starting to reflect that emphasis. Sophomore right guard Tyler Booker (6-5, 335) was a PFF Freshman All-American last year and Bama expects him to be a difference maker in the run game. The Tide expect a similar run-blocking jump from right tackle JC Latham (6-5, 335) who started 13 games last year. Latham was a dominant pass protector, allowing only one hit on the quarterback and no sacks on 486 pass blocking snaps. Expect Latham to vie with Notre Dame's Joe Alt for the first tackle off of the board in the 2024 NFL Draft. A similar upgrade is expected at left tackle with former five star recruit Elijah Pritchett. The redshirt freshman is new to the starting lineup, but the 6-6, 310 athlete will infuse the line with athleticism and aggression. Overall, Alabama will be better on both lines of scrimmage.

Weaknesses

The Tide haven't had to worry about their starting quarterback since 2016. After a disappointing Spring from Jalen Milroe and Ty Simpson and an unsuccessful attempt to purchase Drake Maye's transfer from North Carolina (just months after Saban's rant about Texas A&M buying their recruiting class), former Notre Dame offensive coordinator Tommy Rees lured his former quarterback Tyler Buchner to compete for the starting job in Tuscaloosa. Problem solved? Well, maybe. Before Rees took the Alabama job, he chose to try to upgrade Buchner with Wake Forest transfer Sam Hartman. Granted, Hartman is a very good college quarterback, but if Rees were in love with Buchner's skill set he would have committed to his offseason development and certainly wouldn't have put the full court press on Hartman. Perhaps Notre Dame head coach Marcus Freeman mandated that move (at least that's what Rees better have told Buchner) but it is not clear that Alabama's quarterback problem has been definitively solved with a Golden Domed savior who has been more rollercoaster than rock.

3rd year sophomore Jalen Milroe is a powerful 6-2, 220 redshirt sophomore with top notch running ability. He was shaky as a passer in limited action last year and had some deer-in-the-headlights moments in his start against Texas A&M. In all, he threw three interceptions in only 53 passing attempts and averaged a pathetic 5.6 yards per passing attempt. On the positive side, he averaged 8.5 yards per carry, including an impressive 77 yard scamper against Arkansas. Alabama kept the training wheels on him, but Milroe is known as a hard worker and team leader. The new focus in the offense may suit his skill set better and quarterbacks can get better at football over time.

The last time college fans saw Tyler Buchner, he was throwing a pair of pick sixes in a bowl game against South Carolina (he threw three picks overall, but also tossed three touchdowns in the shootout win while rushing for another pair – that's the full Buchner experience). Buchner is a mistake prone passer (6 touchdowns, 8 interceptions over two limited action seasons) but he has a lively arm capable of making inspired throws and is a greatly underestimated runner with legitimate speed, averaging 5.6 yards per carry and totaling 7 rushing touchdowns. Buchner was the starter in South Bend last year, but he missed four months of the season with an AC joint sprain. Notre Dame upgraded with Sam Hartman, but that doesn't mean that Buchner won't be an upgrade for Alabama.

Redshirt freshman Ty Simpson may have the highest upside as a pocket passer, but inexperience means that he's unlikely to be the early season starter.

Getting into Saban's brain here is essential. Saban wants to run the ball and embrace play action. Both Millroe and Buchner are good runners and they can both credibly execute the passing offense if protected. Saban now has two athletic quarterbacks that he can run to create a more diverse offensive threat and if one of them gets hurt, he will shrug and go with #2. Getting Buchner may have had less to do with upgrading Milroe than simply having two assets that he can break. The one who makes the least mistakes in Fall camp will start, but Saban isn't shy about benching starting quarterbacks. He's done it in-season multiple times and he's done it in a national title game.

NFL draft boards tout talented cornerback Kool-Aid Mckinstry as a future first round pick and he deserves those accolades, but the sophomore cornerback struggled with elite route runners in man coverage last year, repeatedly demonstrating that one of his key ingredients is a big scoop of pass interference. The rest of the Alabama secondary will have real questions after losing three NFL draft picks and having to turn to the portal for FBS replacement level starter Trey Amos from Louisiana at left cornerback while elevating redshirt freshman Earl Little to nickel to join true freshman strong safety Micah Downs. Pairing two freshmen in the secondary, no matter how physically gifted, will not be without some early season bumps and bruises. Senior Malachi Moore will be there to coordinate the back end at free safety and he is a high level player. The smart money says that Alabama's secondary remains vulnerable to high level passing games and they will rely on pass rush to disguise their inexperience.

WYOMING COWBOYS

September 16 | Austin, TX

2022 RECORD	POINTS SCORED	POINTS ALLOWED
7-6	21.2	23.9
Not Ranked	#110 of 131	#48 of 131

MOUNTAIN WEST CONFERENCE
Craig Bohl | 10th season
2022 conference record 5-3

RETURNING STARTERS
OFFENSE - 5 | DEFENSE - 5

Overview

Beautiful Wyoming is the ninth largest state in the United States at 98,000 square miles, but dead last in population at just around 500,000 citizens. That ratio means that if the entire population of the state played zone defense from border to border, you would have only five defenders per square mile. Over half of them would be women, children and old people. This brings up the obvious question – in 2022, could Quinn Ewers and Xavier Worthy have completed a deep ball somewhere in Wyoming?

Speaking of population density, after a rough offseason in the transfer portal, roster numbers are a problem for the Wyoming football team. They're going to have to cowboy up in Laramie. The Wyoming Cowboys posted a winning 7-6 record last year (their 3rd winning record in the last 4) but rather than return a dangerous team that would have been legitimate Mountain West contenders and a big problem for anyone visiting Laramie's 7,200 foot elevation, other programs combed through the Cowboy roster from December through May like they were a 2nd grader getting a lice treatment. Their losses include:

Their most talented offensive lineman Emmanuel Pregnon to USC, where he will start at guard.

Leading wide receiver Joshua Cobbs to Houston.

Their best edge Oluwaseyi Omotosho to Oregon State.

Cam Stone and Keonte Glinton – former starting corner and nickel, respectively – to New Mexico State and Hawaii.

They also lost #1 rusher Titus Swen after a suspension. Swen was the brightest skill position spot on an otherwise moribund Cowboy offense. Their second best returning running back and bowl starter Jordan Vaughn also entered the portal.

Portal traffic isn't a one lane street even on the most desolate highway between Cheyenne and Casper, but Wyoming's off season bounty wasn't stellar. They lost more than they gained. Their best portal win was Northern Illinois running back Harrison Waylee. He rushed for 1,929 yards over 22 games for the Huskies and he will be Wyoming's 190 pound bell cow. Waylee is quick and explosive, but he has a history of nagging injuries due to his lack of size. Less impressive grabs were a backup wide receiver from Vanderbilt and a 4th string quarterback from Iowa. If you have watched Iowa play offense, being the 4th string quarterback in Iowa City is like being the worst dentist in Oklahoma.

That's life for the Group of 5 teams now. They are farm and ranch leagues for the major conferences and while program loyalty or unique environments may keep a few stalwarts around, the siren's song of NIL cash and a bigger stage makes the exodus of emerging talents nearly assured. Wyoming actually has good facilities for their level, but no native recruiting base, geographical isolation and the occasional dip in temperature to -25 degrees isn't the best lure for athletes from Texas and California.

Wyoming head coach Craig Bohl is trying to drive cattle through a NIL landscape stocked with well-armed Power 5 bandits and Comanches when he already had plenty to worry about with flooded river crossings, gopher holes and mountain lions. After a tough rebuild in Laramie nine years ago where he went 6-18 in his first two years, he made the Cowboys a winner, securing five bowl games and five winning seasons in his last seven. Bohl has long been a respected defensive mind but he is amusingly conservative (he went for it on 4th down only 7 times last year – Texas Tech exceeded that number in one game against Texas) but the Cowboys are generally a lock to play smart fundamental defense and give it their all for a full 60 minutes.

Texas gets Wyoming at the right time – the week after what should be a mentally and physically draining trip to Alabama; a nice reset before opening conference play at Baylor. Wyoming also happens to be the season opening opponent for the Texas Tech Red Raiders and that game in Laramie may be an interesting measuring stick for the Horns a couple of weeks later. It's always dangerous for Texas to use the transitive property of common opponent scores because it doesn't really compare apples to apples. It's dangerous for Texas Tech to employ the transitive property because they probably assume it has something to do with an illegal camp of transsexuals.

The Wyoming Cowboys will be competitive against their Mountain West peers and they will show true grit in Laramie, but they're coming to Austin for a 1.85 million dollar Venmo payment and an L.

Strengths

The Cowboys hung their hats on gritty defense last year and will do so again. They didn't turn opponents over – nabbing only 6 interceptions in 13 games – but they did a good job of preventing big plays and held opponents to only 5.4 yards per play. They also had a knack for devising game plans against one trick pony offenses, which is how they upset a ten win Air Force and nearly took down Boise State. The most diverse and competent offenses they played last year – BYU led by QB Jaren Hall – had no trouble slicing them up for 38 points and 500+ yards. There is not a lot that Wyoming can do against multifaceted offensive speed in the passing game but play zone, limit big plays, and hope that opposing receivers and quarterbacks can't get on the same page or fizzle out in the red zone.

The best Wyoming talent is in their front six. They notched 37 sacks last year, a testament to their ability to get after the passer. They have three defensive players who would likely be on the Longhorn two deep and they will be eager to test themselves against Texas. Three year starting nose tackle Cole Godbout is a 6-4, 290 pound rugged run stopper and high motor athlete. He plays bigger than he is and he has great play strength. Linebacker Easton Gibbs (121 tackles, 3 sacks, 9 tackles for loss in 2022) is a former high school quarterback turned middle linebacker tackling machine. Think of a classic Gary Patterson linebacker conversion and that's Gibbs. Easton has good lateral movement and he flies to contact. Edge DeVonne Harris is a pass rushing specialist who notched 8 sacks last year, but he's a 6-4, 230 finesse edge who will struggle to hold up against the run. He will cause a lot of mischief in the Mountain West this year, but Kelvin Banks will put him in time out.

Kicker John Hoyland is one of the best special teams assets in America. He went 22 of 25 last year and was perfect on PATs, hitting four field goal attempts over 50 yards. His big leg wasn't just bolstered by Laramie's thin air altitude. Given his legitimate range out to 55 yards and Wyoming's poor offense, the Cowboys aren't too shy about playing for field goal attempts once they cross the opponent 40 yard line.

Weaknesses

Last year, Wyoming was ranked as the 100th best team in the country by advanced statistics FEI modeling. This team looks comparable. They certainly have a smattering of players that could play for and contribute at Texas, but that number can be counted on the right hand of a shop teacher who spends too much time around the bandsaw. Wyoming is a proud program, but it's important to remember the larger context of what a middling Mountain West team actually is.

Offensively, Wyoming was abysmal last year. They ranked 115th in the country in efficiency metrics, scored 21.2 points per game and managed only 5.2 yards per play. They ran the ball quite effectively behind a pretty good offensive line (they average a very healthy 4.9 yards per carry), but that offensive line has now graduated, transferred or is recovering from offseason surgeries. Instead of returning four starters and six of their top eight offensive linemen, they find themselves perilously thin. Imagine starting a Wyoming winter in December of 2022 snug in a thick parka of offensive linemen and by February 2023 you're stripped down to Fruit of The Looms and the mesh half shirt that Scott Glenn wore in Urban Cowboy.

The Wyoming passing game was a nightmare and it doesn't look like it will improve much. It is difficult to find a traditional non-option based offense that throws for only 126 yards a game, but that's Wyoming. Like a Cheyenne bride's errant fart, perhaps they can blame it on the harsh prairie wind. Expect tight end Treyton Welch to be the primary target of the passing game in 2023. The 240 pound 2nd team All Mountain West tight end started his career as a 190 pound wide receiver and 50 pounds later he still moves like a wide out. Unfortunately for Wyoming, quarterback Andrew Peasley was one of the worst starting quarterbacks in FBS. Peasley gave Cowboy fans palsy, completing only 52% of his passes while averaging an atrocious 5.7 yards per attempt. He had nearly as many interceptions as touchdowns (10 TD, 9 INT) and the Cowboy throw game was primarily reduced to the quick game and single read bootleg play action. He's a decent running threat, mostly because Wyoming would rather have him try to run for five yards rather than try to throw for ten.

Backup Jayden Clemons was worse than Peasley, throwing three interceptions in only 29 attempts in his two starts. In the offseason, head coach Craig Bohl wisely brought in several transfer quarterbacks, but it's unclear whether any represent an upgrade. If Wyoming is smart, they'll have a wealthy cattle rancher try to buy Maalik Murphy's services during pregame warm ups with a beef futures contract and vague promises of rights to a uranium mine.

The Wyoming secondary has some experience but will struggle to match up against higher end athletes, so expect a steady dose of zone and off coverages. Texas' ability to pile up points will depend on execution, finishing drives and taking easy yardage. They can't run with the Longhorns so they will try to confuse Ewers and stop one play scoring drives.

BAYLOR BEARS
September 23 | Waco, TX

2022 RECORD	POINTS SCORED	POINTS ALLOWED
6-7	32.2	26.8
Not Ranked	#39 of 131	#69 of 131

BIG XII CONFERENCE
Dave Aranda | 4th season
2022 conference record 4-5

RETURNING STARTERS
OFFENSE - 3 | DEFENSE - 5

Overview

Baylor's football program is very beta. Not in the sense that they are subordinate males who cook breakfast for their wife's boyfriend on Sunday mornings or sit on window seats sipping chai soys while scrolling through Pinterest, but rather in the financial industry sense of beta as a measurement of volatility and systemic risk. Actually, having met a few Baylor fans, I may also mean the first part, but let's talk about the second.

Baylor is a high beta program with yearly swings so wild that this team has become nearly impossible to predict. Since 2015, the program is somehow always simultaneously in decay while blossoming with renewal. Baylor takes the predictable circle of life that governs most programs and turns it into the rhombus of guessing. Baylor is lukewarm in the way that the water runoff from a volcano erupting onto a glacier is tepid. If one of those forces shifts, you don't want to be in the water.

Since 2015, the Baylor Bears have had four different head football coaches and their seasons have gone thusly:

2015 Art Briles 10-3 (6-3 B12)

2016 Jim Grobe 7-6 (3-6 B12)

2017 Matt Rhule 1-11 (1-8 B12)

2018 Matt Rhule 7-6 (4-5 B12)

2019 Matt Rhule 11-3 (8-1 B12)

2020 Dave Aranda 2-7 (2-7 B12)

2021 Dave Aranda 12-2 (7-2 B12)

2022 Dave Aranda 6-7 (4-5 B12)

That's a 35-37 regular season Big 12 conference record. Over that span, their win differentials were -3, -6, +6, +4, -9, +10, -6. Those numbers comprise an aggregate season record of 56-45. A 55% winning percentage suggests middling program consistency and reliable mediocrity. What a lie. Every year, Baylor is either really good, atrocious, or mind numbingly average.

But…wait a minute. Aren't those the potential results for any program in any given year? No, not really. Not like that. Such extremes don't follow each other in whiplash see-saw succession. Most programs follow fairly predictable patterns of ramp up, reset, decline, ramp up with modest variation over time. Since 2015, Baylor's mean win differential has varied by more than 6 wins per season. No other team in college football comes close.

Last season, many in the media dutifully filled in their ballots for Baylor to win the league again because it happened in 2021 (thus, it should happen again – science!) as cursory study revealed that they returned many of their starters. They neglected to examine the actual personnel that Baylor lost. Who was responsible for the actual winning and who was a role player? Michael Jordan and Luc Longley shared three NBA championships in Chicago. Might one of them have exerted a tad more influence on those results than the other? 2021 Baylor won in a very specific manner with the league's best defense, a strong running game and a deep threat pass catcher. When each leg of that stool is sawed away, one is left sitting on a round piece of wood and the bartender can't see you.

Baylor lost six NFL draft picks from their 2021 Big 12 title team, four of them going in the first three rounds of the draft, most of them deployed at the key positions that made Baylor's defense work. They also lost their two big play offensive/special teams impact players and several key contributors who fit what Baylor does, even if the NFL didn't love them. Georgia can endure those losses with a shrug. Baylor cannot. Remember this when we preview TCU. *Foreshadowing!*

So the consensus pick to win the league went 4-5 in Big 12 play and dropped six wins from their prior season total. A similar whiplash variance happened in 2020, as Matt Rhule lost four critical players to the NFL draft and several more 5th and 6th year starters from his outstanding 2019 team. That was a nine win drop off! Rhule understood the nature of his roster losses and had already begun his job search, demonstrating that job timing is the most critical underrated skill a head coach can cultivate. Rhule also stopped recruiting and that had implications for his successor.

Dave Aranda chose a different path after his white hot 2021 popularity, ignoring rapturous courting by other programs and negotiating a contract extension through 2029. While Rhule sought a rung up the ladder, Aranda chose to use his leverage to build an unassailable nest of security. There is no easy parting for either Baylor or Aranda now, though his specific contract details are opaque as Baylor is a private institution. That means they do not have to disclose employee information, contract structures, the details of Brazos style Eyes Wide Shut parties, or whether it's true that 37% of Waco's economy is just youth pastors running

Herbalife multi-level marketing pyramid schemes. These things are likely all true, but this preview cannot engage in irresponsible speculation.

Aranda may have built some security, but that didn't apply to his staff. After 2022's disappointment, Aranda fired defensive coordinator (and his former mentor) Ron Roberts and harvested safeties/special teams coach Ronnie Wheat. Given that those were the areas where Baylor was most deficient, it makes sense, but Aranda is a defensive coach with significant input on that side of the ball and Roberts was the titular defensive coordinator when Baylor fielded a dominant 2021 defense. Were these fired coaches non-performers or fall guys? Or did Aranda take his eye off of his beloved defense and realize that the only way to set it right was to roll up his sleeves and get his hands dirty again? Baylor brings back former safeties coach Matt Powledge (his last name combines both power and knowledge) from Oregon to fill both roles and provide the answer.

The Bears also play a remarkable 8 home games, a function of scheduling my son's flag football team as part of their non-conference schedule. Can Aranda right the ship on defense while judiciously using the portal to rebuild the offense and have another breakout? That scenario is perfectly plausible. If the recent and erratic past is any indication, Baylor will probably do something great or terrible. Perhaps the real surprise would be achieving what looks like the most probable outcome: a respectable winning season, powered by a forgiving conference slate where Texas and Texas Tech travel to Waco and they get to play three conference newcomers and West Virginia.

If things fall right, this looks like an eight win quality bowl team capable of beating any team in the league on the right Saturday. If things don't fall quite right, Baylor is capable of looking pretty awful, reinforcing rumors that it was former Baylor staffer Joey McGuire who was responsible for Baylor's mental readiness on game day. Last year, the bad version of Baylor lost 43-40 to West Virginia and they were mercilessly dominated by Air Force in their bowl game, getting doubled up in time of possession and going 0/11 of 3rd down.

It should shock no one that the 2023 Baylor Bears are a football team with a wide range of prospective outcomes. They return only eight starters overall, but replacing losing players with better players is not a bad thing. Did they though?

Strengths

Defensive ends Gabe Hall and TJ Franklin return as 5th year seniors and multi-year starters. The 6-6, 300 pound Hall is a very good player who Texas fans will remember for sacking and stripping Quinn Ewers for a 16 yard rumbling touchdown last year. He has 10.5 sacks over the last two years and possesses ideal strength and length for the 4i position, a technique where Baylor lines up its end heads up on the offensive tackle. Meanwhile, TJ Franklin disappointed last year and refocused in the offseason to getting back to the level of play that he exhibited in years previous. Franklin got in better shape and should be more impactful in his final season after 32 career starts. Baylor loses big Siaki Ika at nose tackle to the NFL, but Baylor faithful contend that big Louisiana Tech transfer Jerrell Boykins (6-3, 345) will be a more than adequate replacement. Boykins has only played JUCO ball (he redshirted at Louisiana Tech) and if he doesn't live up to the hype, the Bears may be forced to move Hall inside if young Tre Emory can't step up in his stead. Edge Garmon Randolph is a long 6-7, 250 and though he secured 4.5 sacks last year, Baylor coaches believe that he is capable of much more in their scheme.

The Bear running backs should be good. Big 12 Freshman Offensive Player of the Year Richard Reese is back after rushing for 972 yards and 14 touchdowns. The 5-9, 175 pound back runs with courage and excellent quickness and is capable of 25-30 carry afternoons when needed. Fortunately, Baylor does have Oklahoma State transfer Dominic Richardson to complement Reese and prevent the tread from going entirely off of the tire. Richardson is a no-frills runner who ran for 543 yards last year in Stillwater, but he averaged a pedestrian 3.6 yards per carry despite his 8 touchdowns. His longest run of the year went for only 19 yards, but Richardon's running style was not well suited to a Cowboy line that got little push up front. Despite Richardson's lack of explosiveness toting the rock, he is a very capable receiver, grabbing 29 balls over his Cowboy career. The final piece in a three-headed backfield is Qualan Jones. The 5-10, 245 pound runner is pretty much just thighs and shoulder pads coming through the hole and he totaled 462 yards rushing at 5 yards per carry with 7 touchdowns as their primary short yardage runner and goal line back. Despite his power profile, Jones has nice hands (23 catches last year) and he is capable of maximizing a well blocked run.

Baylor added players in the portal to bolster their strength on both sides of the ball and they are counting on at least seven of them to start. Center Clark Barrington transferred from

BYU to Baylor and he is considered a later round NFL talent. He'll stabilize the interior and should contend for All-Big 12 honors. His little brother Campbell Barrington (if 6-6, 305 is little) followed him from BYU and he should start at left tackle. Campbell started for BYU as a true freshman but was benched as a sophomore before breaking his thumb midseason, so it's not entirely clear what the Bears are getting. Given that Baylor offensive coordinator Jeff Grimes and offensive line coach Eric Mateos coached both players in Provo, they probably understand exactly what they're getting.

In addition to the big nose tackle from Louisiana Tech being counted on to start, they also added Liberty middle linebacker Mike Smith to replace the hard-hitting Dillon Doyle. Smith is a smaller speed linebacker who led the Flames in tackles last year. The Bears also added pass rusher and blitz linebacker Byron Vaughns from Utah State (and former Texas Longhorn) and in two years there he totaled 19 tackles for loss and 6.5 sacks. He should contribute heavily in the rotation and isn't a bad bet for a breakout candidate after gaining 20 pounds of good weight in the offseason. Finally, Baylor added cornerback Isaiah Dunson from Miami. Dunson is a big press corner who never broke into the starting lineup in Coral Gables. Aside from Blake Shapen's improvement at quarterback, the simplest bellwether indicator for Baylor season success is predicated on whether or not their portal transfers hit. If yes, they should be pretty good. If not? It will be a long season in Waco.

Weaknesses

Baylor returns only one starter in their secondary. Historically, defensive backfield experience is a very telling leading indicator for their unit success, but it could be argued that Aranda gave at least one of these guys their walking papers. There could have been four returning starters but starting safety Devin Neal left for Louisville and Arkansas plucked cornerback Lorando Johnson and big nickel Al Walcott from Waco. Walcott was 2nd Team All Big 12 for the Bears and their best turnover creator. Baylor will try to fill in the gaps with transfers and homegrown talent, but inexperience at defensive back guarantees some growing pains. They will also try out an interesting permutation at their nickel spot, using 6th year senior and pass rush specialist 6-2, 205 pound Bryson Jackson as an edge blitzer and general disruptor. This is Aranda trying to recreate what he had with former Big 12 Defensive Player of the Year Jalen Pitre, who was an exceptional blitzer, but Pitre could also cover receivers and do almost anything he was asked. Can Jackson?

Quarterback Blake Shapen currently doesn't belong as a weakness or strength. He has shown flashes of both good and bad as a starter, but the redshirt junior has to elevate the passing offense if Baylor wants to shake out of offensive mediocrity. Shapen threw for 2709 yards last year at a moderate 7.4 yards per attempt while completing over 63% of his passes. He also threw 10 interceptions to go with his 18 passing touchdowns and against quality defenses, Baylor struggled badly to get the ball down the field. Their checkdown offense was a byproduct of Shapen's inconsistency, but a mediocre and inconsistent Baylor receiving corps also bears much of the blame. This year, returning starters Monaray Baldwin (33 catches, 564 yards) and Hal Pressley (32 grabs for 382 yards) are joined by Arkansas transfer Ketron Jackson (career total: 21 catches, 374 yards, 4 touchdowns last year) and the trio must be more consistent and provide tangible downfield threats for Baylor's play action offense to fully prosper.

Monaray Baldwin is small and fast at 5-10, 160 pounds (10.5 100 meters in high school) and while Baylor media and national publications are playing up Ketron Jackson as a former SEC dominator, the hard truth is that he was KJ Jefferson's fifth receiving option and has looked like Tarzan but played like Jane. North Texas tight end transfer Jake Roberts is an intriguing addition. He started 37 games in Denton and snagged 28 balls last year. Penciling in 35-40 catches for him in this offense makes sense. Bottom line: the entire Baylor passing game has to improve markedly so that they can unleash a talented backfield.

Baylor has recruited adequately under Dave Aranda after a tough start and they've been fairly adept at filling needs to their system on both sides of the ball, but Matt Rhule stopped recruiting when he realized he was leaving and a staff that could read the tea leaves wasn't spending Friday nights at a La Quinta in East Texas wooing recruits. On3 ranked Baylor's 2020 recruiting class 50th in the nation and aside from starting guard Gavin Byers and Blake Shapen, every member of that class has proven undistinguished, busted or transferred out. As Texas Longhorn fans can attest, busting on an entire class irrespective of ranking sets back program continuity and can handicap a staff for years. The portal and subsequent recruiting classes allowed Baylor to make up ground, but the Bears will need another year before they can fully shake off the impact of that roster hit.

KANSAS JAYHAWKS

September 30 | Austin, TX

BIG XII CONFERENCE
Lance Leipold | 3rd season
2022 conference record 3-6

2022 RECORD	**POINTS SCORED**	**POINTS ALLOWED**
6-7	35.6	35.5
Not Ranked	#21 of 131	#124 of 131

RETURNING STARTERS
OFFENSE - 10 | DEFENSE - 7

Overview

Last season, Lance Leipold's coaching and the emergence of multiple offensive threats enabled by a creative RPO driven offense propelled Kansas to a 6-6 regular season record and a heartbreaking 55-53 bowl loss to Arkansas. They even finished ranked in the top 50 with respect to total team advanced metrics, which had not happened since 2008. No easy task when your defense is ranked 104th in the country. There are few schools in America where a 6-7 record and a close bowl loss are cause for celebration, but in Lawrence the enthusiasm is off of the charts. OK, that's not true. That was irresponsible preview hyperbole. Their excitement is on the chart, but still pretty high on the Y axis. It is not like the enthusiasm Jayhawk fans have when the hoops team looks good in an intramural scrimmage, but people are pretty upbeat about KU football. They have every right to be.

That 6 game win total eclipsed the total program wins for the Jayhawks over the prior three years combined. From 2010-2021, the Jayhawks have been 23-118 (a 16.3% winning percentage) and had two winless seasons. Averaging less than two wins per year will tend to deflate a fan base that already prefers bouncy round balls to prolate spheroids, but the apathy and defeatism in Lawrence was at Communist Bloc levels, the sort of spirit-crushing despair one only experiences dealing with a HOA or reading a 38 year old New York City woman's Twitter.

A journey is measured in the distance traveled and no college football program progressed more than the Jayhawks. Credit Leipold's vision, credit the players, but credit the Kansas administration for finally learning the hard lesson to hire a hungry competent football coach who clawed his way up the ranks at Wisconsin-Whitewater and Buffalo rather than hiring another media and agent driven PR candidate like Turner Gill, Charlie Weis or Les Miles. There is a distinct difference between a has-been coach trying to pad their retirement accounts and get the down payment for a lake house at their last coaching stop versus a hungry coach with a major chip on their shoulder trying to create a legacy.

Lance Leipold had a terrific run at Division III Wisconsin-Whitewater (a college or a rafting trip?) where he went 109-6 with six national championships. He then coached Buffalo to football relevance in the MAC conference going 37-33 over six years, twice earning MAC Coach of the Year honors. Leipold is a real honest-to-goodness football coach and proof that there are quality leaders at every level of the game just waiting for their shot.

What about the Jayhawk team?

The Jayhawks return the most starters in the entire league (17) including ten starters on an offense that was the most explosive on a per play basis in the Big 12, every one of their consequential skill players, the most proven quarterback room in the league (fight me) and an extraordinary 91% of their offensive production.

Defensively, the Jayhawks will…field eleven men on defense. If they could field twelve, they might actually be pretty good. Alas, this is illegal and would draw a penalty. Trust me, Lance Leipold checked on that. Jabs at the Kansas defense are well-deserved, but they can't get worse. And they could actually field a passable secondary (technically, they want a non-passable secondary, right?) if a couple of transfers pan out to complement two or three returning quality starters. Their linebackers are also now nearing league average. If the defensive line can improve from a nuclear disaster zone to merely a fly-infested landfill, then Kansas can win some more games 33-31 instead of losing them 45-38.

Leipold's cultural build out didn't allow big program poachers to swoop in and rob a promising nucleus of skill athletes who could start or contribute significantly at several bigger name programs. How did they pull that off? Maybe Bill Self diverted some basketball cash their way, but the more likely answer is that the Kansas players are invested. Individual players were willing to pass on greener pastures to complete a shared team journey out of the cellar to, well, if not the penthouse, to a townhome with running water and no squatters. That sort of unity of purpose should focus our attention and it's one of the few intangibles where this preview places tangible credence.

I won't oversell the Jayhawks as their structural weaknesses are apparent and bad injury luck would expose them completely, but middling teams – which will be most of the 2023 Big 12 – are not going to enjoy playing Kansas one bit. If you want an early tell on the Jayhawks and their ability to shore up their weaknesses, pay close attention to a September 8th home stand against Illinois. Brett Bielema's offense is 100% smashmouth and if the Kansas defense shows more physicality and run-stopping ability, the Jayhawks may be more than a heartwarming underdog story.

Strengths

Quarterback Jalon Daniels is the conduit for the Jayhawk offense with a mind as quick as his feet. He averaged a generous 8.8 yards per attempt last year and threw 18 touchdowns to only 4 interceptions before injuries forced him out of the lineup for four weeks. Daniels is an excellent run threat (425 yards rushing, 5.5 yards per carry, 7 rushing touchdowns), but he does his primary damage through the air on a variety of downfield vertical play action reads that require deft ball handling as much as accuracy and immediate recognition. When Daniels went down last year, backup signal caller Jason Bean stepped up and showed nearly approximate passing skills to Daniels (Bean passed for 14 touchdowns against 4 interceptions) to go along with his 10.36 100 meter speed that garnered him a 5.8 yards per carry average and another 4 rushing touchdowns. In aggregate, the Jayhawk quarterbacks accounted for 11 rushing touchdowns, 32 passing touchdowns and over 3900 yards of total offense. Not bad. Somehow, Kansas convinced Bean to return again for a sixth season despite starting offers from other Power Five schools.

They also return the starting receiver trio of Grimm, Skinner and Arnold – who combined for 15 receiving touchdowns – and further complement them with giant TE Mason Fairchild (6 touchdown catches) who has a surprising knack for getting loose downfield despite weighing 265+ pounds and having a diet consisting only of Belgian waffles. None of these four pass catchers are individually remarkable, but they are all good players and in aggregate they are terrifying to the average FBS secondary. Stopping the Kansas RPO game is an exercise in whack-a-mole. Rounding out the bunch is 6-0, 255 pound hybrid tight end/fullback Jared Casey who caught 16 balls for 218 yards and 3 touchdowns last year, including a 66 yard score against Texas Tech. Casey is a physical lead blocker and he's just agile enough to slip into the flat and make a play in the passing game. Texas fans may remember him as the former walk-on who caught the two point conversion in Austin to beat Texas 57-56 in Sark's first year. Sorry. Didn't mean to bring that memory back.

Running back Devin Neal is a solid run maximizer who quietly amassed over 1,000 rushing yards at a healthy 6.1 yards per clip with a physical don't-quit running style that evokes former Longhorn Roschon Johnson. 17% of his carries went for 10+ yards, which is outstanding. They even bring back backup scat back Daniel Hinshaw, who averaged 6 yards a carry and scored 6 touchdowns.

That strange feeling in your stomach is the dawning realization that the Jayhawk skill players are easily in the league's top quartile and arguably the second best bunch overall behind Texas. They come in waves, they have multiple players at every position and they're smart enough to understand the leverage points in the Kansas RPO offense, They make very few mental mistakes despite the multitude of motions, formations and trickery that the Jayhawks engage in to disguise a half dozen core plays. The thought of Kansas with better skill talent than most of the league is heretical to casual fans, but 1). It's true and 2). Averaging 7.0 yards per play last year requires dudes. Kansas has dudes. It's Call of Dudey in Lawrence.

Kansas also has a few dudes in their secondary. Kansas safety Kenny Logan returns again as their leading tackler, his 5th year as a starter at safety. Logan is a physical player who supports the run enthusiastically but he has below average coverage instincts as a keep-the-top-on safety. Why he was tabbed as the free safety last year is a mystery, but it's important that the Jayhawks get him closer to the line of scrimmage and away from trying to run with fly routes. Cornerback Cobee Bryant will be one of the elite corners in the conference and while he's not The Black Mamba, he's at least an angry coral snake. Bryant is a feast or famine gambler on the corner, but their defense will trade turnover creation and aggression for the occasional toasting. Corner Mello Dotson is exactly the kind of overlooked three star Florida athlete who always blossoms late in his college career. Finally, linebacker/nickel hybrid Craig Young, a former Ohio State transfer, has the requisite physical ability (he's a 10.7 100 meters guy at 225 pounds) but his play hasn't matched his measurables.

Weaknesses

Kansas has some work to do on a defense that gave up 30+ points nine times in 13 games. The unit gave up 469 yards per game, allowed opponents to convert 50% of 3rd and 4th downs combined and gave up 35 points per game (124th nationally). The absence of quality defensive linemen backed by Kansas linebackers that couldn't escape blocking attention was much of the problem, but the secondary had some very toasty moments as well. They stopped runs like laxative-laced chili and dropping an extra man in the box to thwart the ground game allowed big plays over the top. As the season progressed, they were injured and plain worn out in addition to being bad. Offenses like Oklahoma, Texas, Arkansas and Kansas State brutally manhandled them in the running game. Something has to change if Kansas wants to elevate from a scrappy peripheral bowl team.

Kansas worked in the offseason to bring in some bodies to clog up running lanes and provide some semblance of a pass rush. Some of them were clear depth and developmental additions from Minnesota (former Gopher Gage Keys might start though) and Utah State, but the most promising transfer is Colorado State defensive tackle Devin Phillips. Phillips has 36 career starts and is considered a quality run stopper. He was a big get for a defense seeking simple competence up front. The homegrown solutions need to get better as well. It's imperative that Kansas interior returnee Tommy Dunn and edge rusher Jereme Robinson raise their games and their offseason lifts after showing some flashes of potential in 2022. Kansas should be improved here, but a traffic cone wearing shoulder pads would be an improvement.

It's not all on the defensive line. Kansas linebacker Rich Miller is an active tackler, but he has to be much more consistent. His sidekick Taiwan Berryhill needs to stop embracing a One China policy, quit running around blocks, and face down the threat in front of him. Kansas defensive coordinator Brian Borland, who has been professionally married to Lance Leipold for decades, has to deploy his assets more creatively on the back end. Kenny Logan is a box safety and the Jayhawk corners are better in man than zone. Scheme it up accordingly, Coach Borland.

Much is rightly written about the Kansas skill personnel on offense, but the difference between real football and fantasy football is that the five guys up front matter. The Jayhawk offensive line is seasoned and boasts four returning starters each with between 4-6 years of college tenure. Transfers from places as disparate as Wisconsin, Buffalo, Louisville and Central Missouri. On the whole, they are not physically elite (though Wiscy transfer Logan Brown was a former big-time recruit) and Kansas schemes them up to advantage without asking too much. Most defensive lines in the league won't be able to exploit them, but when they go against the league's elite they will be challenged. The best tactic for Kansas

offensive line play is to play together in a clever system that relieves them of the pressure to dominate the man in front of them. So why are they listed as a weakness? Injuries or any fall off in play would be terminal to Kansas' dreams of a bowl season. The dropoff in quality from a Kansas offensive line starter to backup is precipitous.

OKLAHOMA SOONERS
October 7 | Dallas, TX

2022 RECORD	POINTS SCORED	POINTS ALLOWED
6-7	32.8	30
Not Ranked	#33 of 131	#99 of 131

BIG XII CONFERENCE
Brent Venables | 2nd season
2022 conference record 3-6

RETURNING STARTERS
OFFENSE - 5 | DEFENSE - 7

Overview

The Oklahoma Sooners started the 2022 season well enough. Ranked 6th in the country, boasting a 3-0 record against three feeble non-conference opponents (UTEP, Kent State and Nebraska would finish with a combined 14-22 record) that they outscored an average of 42-10, rookie head coach Brent Venables' team entered their late September home conference opener against Kansas State with the confident appearance of a Big 12 title contender; yet another Sooner team that would breeze its way to double digit wins. At least that's how it looked to anyone who hadn't watched them play and just scanned the box scores. The Sooner defense was cutting corners with cheap pressure against terrible offenses and the Sooner offense, though pretty good, struggled at times to do simple things. At this juncture, the writer of this preview may have engaged in legal gambling to short the Sooners and exploit betting lines distorted by their false image of elite quality.

Three hours after the first whistle in their Big 12 opener, the Sooners had their first loss of the season. The losses kept on coming, low lighted by a 55-24 destruction at the hands of TCU, a vicious decimation by their most hated rival in Dallas 49-0, and an inexplicable late season road loss to a dying West Virginia. The Sooners finished the year losing 7 out of their last 10 games and went 3-6 in Big 12 play. Their season best performance was a 35-32 loss to Florida State in the Cheez-It Bowl but historically great programs don't do moral victories in bowl games named after crackers.

Last year was a sickening spiral, the likes of which Sooner fans hadn't experienced since John Blake's disastrous 1998 denouement. Or that time when they got their Jet Ski repossessed for failure to make minimum payments. For a program accustomed to winning with great teams, good teams and even pretty average teams that somehow found a way, 2022 was a shock to the Sooner system. Since 2000, the Sooners have finished the year with double digit season wins eighteen times and ranked in the postseason AP Top 10 another sixteen times. Hate the Sooners all you like, but that's remarkable consistency and program strength.

Fortunately for Brent Venables – whose Pentecostal motivational speaker on a weekend meth binge vibe creates energy and unease in equal measure – suffering Sooner fans were more than happy to put the lion's share of blame for 2022's woes on departed head coach Lincoln Riley. If hell hath no fury like a woman scorned, when it comes to Riley, the Sooner fan base are screeching harpies. While Oklahoma fell into despair, Riley elevated a 4-8 USC football team to 11-3 with the help of stolen Sooner quarterback Caleb Williams, the Heisman winner and soon-to-be #1 pick in the NFL draft. The Sooners are now a chunky angry girl who just saw their handsome ex marry a rich model heiress to the Jenny Craig fortune and everyone unlucky enough to be on her Facebook feed has to hear about it non-stop. Tough break, Sooners.

Here rests an odd dichotomy. Riley may have indeed been the architect of the Sooner structural woes that finally showed up in 2022, but his offensive genius is the reason that those deficiencies never forced a reckoning. By leaving Oklahoma, Riley left the poison and took the antidote. Riley also deprived Oklahoma of a Heisman winning quarterback who would have certainly one-man ganged the Sooners into more shootout wins, allowing Venables time to turn over his roster without a seven loss season.

Riley's coaching had been masking some deeper program issues. Past Thinking Texas Football previews pointed out that Lincoln Riley hasn't loved his roster for a while now and many forget that he actively lobbied to cancel the entire 2020 football season. His flight to USC proved it. This was reminiscent of Urban Meyer's flight from Florida, except that Riley didn't have to fake a brain cloud. This was a man looking for an exit but there aren't many lateral moves from Oklahoma. Somehow, Riley lucked (and skilled) his way into an upgrade.

Before he left, program malaise showed up in weird and unexpected ways. In 2020, Alex Grinch finally "fixed" the Sooner defense, fielding a Top 10 national unit. In 2021, Oklahoma's defense finished the year ranked #56 in advanced defense metrics despite plenty of returning starters and five defensive stars drafted to the NFL. They underachieved badly on that side of the ball, but Riley's offense covered up the problem. In 2022, Oklahoma finished the season ranked #45 in defensive FEI with a clearly inferior group of athletes to the previous season. That speaks to Venables adjusting on the fly, but it also raises questions about Sooner talent levels and their fit to his new defensive system. At Clemson, Venables was used to having dominant defensive line play with immovable defensive tackles that demanded double teams and 1st round NFL draft pick edge rushers who could get pressure with an honest rush. It's easy to run cool schemes on the back end when your defensive front kicks wholesale ass, but Oklahoma's front was full of Grinch players who got their asses kicked when asked to play without slanting or running risky stunts.

What is clear is that Oklahoma's roster needs turnover. Multiple elite recruits from their 2019 and 2020 classes haven't panned out and the Sooners have been as active jettisoning offseason dead weight as they have been in seeking help at key positions. They must transition their defensive philosophy and their seeming birthright of difference-makers on offense, particularly on the offensive line and at wide receiver, seem in short supply. Lincoln Riley resentment gave Brent Venables some first year cover and Sooner fans, though admittedly worried about their hire's disastrous debut, are at least resigned to giving him a chance to fix the mess. Venables may not be the guy, but judging him solely on last year is unfair.

The Sooner recruiting machine ramped up on the trail and in the portal. The Sooners signed 26 new recruits in a 2023 class that On3 ranked 7th in the nation and have since added an incredible 20 players through the portal. That's not quite Deion Sanders' Colorado levels of turnover, but they remade 55% of their football team in the short span of a few months. Don't accuse Oklahoma of complacency and we should be judicious in forecasting performance from last year to project this year. This is not the same team.

We can do it a little though. Oklahoma lost 5 of their 7 games by a touchdown or less in 2022 and their two blowouts came in games where quarterback Dillon Gabriel missed all or half of the game. The latter statistic is false hope as both of those games would have still been big Sooner losses, but Oklahoma fans need to construct a "we were so close" narrative somehow. Texas fans can relate.

Oklahoma has a highly favorable 2023 schedule with feeble non-conference matchups (SMU, Tulsa, Arkansas State) and the 9th weakest schedule in the Big 12. They will skip out on Texas Tech, Kansas State and Baylor (they were 0-3 against them in 2022) for the

kinder mix of UCF, BYU and Cincinnati. The game against Texas in Dallas looms even larger than usual. Simply injecting some new talent into the program, Year 2 of the new defense and facing a weak schedule guarantees a better 2023 win total, even if the team isn't world-beating. Oklahoma's hopes are pinned on a speedy rebuild engineered by a hotshot but unproven defensive coordinator hire turned head coach. It worked with Bob Stoops 25 years ago. Can they do it again?

New talent, a Charmin soft schedule and pretty good coaches on both sides of the ball means that Oklahoma may not even be all that great and could still make the Big 12 title game. An ogre made out of marshmallows. The silver lining in that scenario?

Texas gets an opportunity to beat them twice in Dallas.

Strengths

The criticisms of Dillon Gabriel as a future NFL quarterback or high level draft prospect are valid. He's small, he has missed multiple games with injury, he has inexplicable fits of inaccuracy on easy throws and he can only throw to certain branches on the route tree. However, Gabriel is unlikely to face the Baltimore Ravens or Dallas Cowboys this year. He plays in college. In that world, over 4 years and 38 starts, he has amassed 11,205 yards passing, 95 touchdowns to only 20 interceptions, a healthy 156.2 career passer rating (he has never been below 154 in any single year) and averages a sizzling 8.8 yards per attempt. The 6 foot standing-on-his-toes signal caller is also mobile and a fine situational runner with 14 career rushing touchdowns. From a macro-perspective, he is a metronome of consistency.

For all of his faults, the failure to see that Gabriel is a dangerous downfield passer who can buy time in the pocket and a seasoned veteran who can get Oklahoma into better plays at the line of scrimmage misunderstands the outsized value of those traits in the college game. Correspondingly, expect Sooner offensive coordinator Jeff Lebby to emphasize Gabriel's strengths, with more emphasis on marrying the running game to play action passing with set piece deep shots or quick one read throws that play well to his skill set. If Gabriel goes down, 5 star recruit Jackson Arnold will take over. He can't be worse than what Oklahoma had behind Gabriel last year and many Sooner fans believe that Arnold is an eventual superstar.

The Sooners lost running back Eric Gray, who excelled behind a quality run blocking offensive line and while Gray's 6.4 yards per carry average and 1300+ rushing yards will be sorely missed, the Sooners, per usual, have an underrated group of candidates to replace him. Jovantae Barnes chipped in 519 yards rushing last year in the #2 role and he will be improved with more offseason work and physical maturation. Barnes hasn't shown game breaking ability, but he is a consistent chain mover. By contrast, young 195 pound Gavin Sawchuk may be the big play runner that OU desires. The youngster will push Barnes hard for reps after starring in the bowl game against Florida State, gaining 100 yards on only 15 carries while repeatedly demonstrating elite instincts and terrific cutting ability. The unit is completed by 230 pound veteran Marcus Major, who returns for his 5th year in Norman. Major is a reliable presence who should serve as their primary short yardage runner and is likely their best pass protector.

The Sooners did non-stop work in the portal this offseason across a range of positions addressing a variety of needs. At least 8 of those portal transfers are guaranteed to start. Is that a testament to the quality of their bounty or to the gaping holes in their roster? Sooner fans think the former, Big 12 fans hope the latter, a game in Dallas in October will reveal the truth.

To shore up a potentially shaky offensive line, they grabbed starting left tackle Walter Rouse from Stanford. Rouse is a graduate transfer with 39 career starts. Joining him on offense is massive 340 pound guard Caleb Shaffer from Miami (Ohio). He has 28 career starts and was 2nd team All-MAC in 2021.The last major pieces are Michigan transfer wide receiver Anthony Andrel, a role player for the Wolverines who caught 8 balls last year and Texas transfer speedster Brenen Thompson, whose spring preference for track over football paved his way to Norman. Tight end Austin Stogner also decided to run it back, opting to return to Oklahoma from South Carolina.

Defensively, they bring in Dasan McCullough, a highly coveted willowy linebacker from Indiana. McCullough will start and should provide a major athletic upgrade to their second level defenders as a pass rusher, sideline to sideline tackler and high level pass defender. Can he stuff a guard when an offense runs right at him, though? 280 pound defensive end Rondell Bothroyd will secure a starting role and the veteran from Wake Forest brings 24.5 tackles for loss over his last two seasons with six sacks last year. Texas Tech transfer safety Reggie Pearson will provide some leadership and direction to the secondary and the 6th year player has 33 career starts.

Was Oklahoma improved by these transfers? Considerably. However, the ease with which so many of them secured starting roles suggests major depth problems and a lack of homegrown options.

Weaknesses

Bill Bedenbaugh is one of the premier offensive line coaches in college football, but the Sooners lost a pair of NFL offensive tackles and two other experienced starters and replaced them with an above average veteran from Stanford at left tackle and redshirt junior Tyler Guyton - a 2021 TCU transfer – at right tackle. Guyton has been inconsistent. The Sooners also had to go to the MAC to find starting guard Caleb Shaffer, who may work out just fine, but this speaks poorly of their on campus options. The other guard spot will probably go to first year starter Savion Byrd, a highly touted recruit from Duncanville who is considered very athletic but not fully formed. Senior center Andrew Raym is back and he has 17 career starts under his belt. He is one of the most overrated players in the league. The Sooners could have a productive offensive line given their coaching, some timely portal work and a Lebby scheme that's favorable to creating space in the running game, but I'm not sold on them as pass protectors or when facing high level defensive lines.

The Sooners seem to always have multiple game breakers at wide receiver, but with the loss of 3rd round deep threat Marvin Mims to the NFL Draft and given the many dry holes drilled on the recruiting trail in years past (due to attitudes, transfers, armed robberies), Oklahoma going to the portal for 3rd string wide receivers from Michigan and Texas to round out their top targets is telling. Fortunately, they do have one high quality asset in Jalil Farooq. The 6-1, 200 pounder has good speed and size and he had 37 catches for 466 yards and 5 touchdowns last year. Expect those numbers to double in 2023 as the Sooners force feed him the ball. Farooq is a terrific runner after the catch and the Sooners will have him carry the ball 1-2 times per game on reverses or jet sweeps. Slot Drake Stoops will start and he's the dictionary definition of a role player, amassing 80 catches over 5 seasons for 914 yards and 7 touchdowns in his career. Typically, Oklahoma has high quality tight ends and pass-catching fullbacks to help carry the passing game load, but they lose underrated playmaker Brayden Willis to the NFL draft. They desperately took three tight ends in the portal and they are hoping that Austin Stogner will return to his 2020 form after his transfer dalliance with South Carolina.

A lack of dangerous threats outside, a smallish quarterback, a revamped offensive line...that can be a volatile combination if the Sooners encounter a defense that can lock down their receivers outside, stop the run and bring pressure. Very few teams on their schedule are constituted well to do that, but I just shared the gameplans for Texas and TCU.

The Sooner run defense must enjoy 24 hour sailing because they sure as hell can't anchor. They were consistently bullied up front and their linebackers struggled to plug the holes in the dam. Giving up 188 yards per game rushing at 4.5 yards per carry isn't good, but the Sooners were actually much worse than that against Big 12 opponents. Over consecutive games during a three game losing streak, Kansas State hit them for 275 yard rushing, TCU drilled them for 361 and Texas dominated for 296. When it looked like the staff had stemmed the bleeding, adjusting their schemes to compensate for their lack of interior mettle, Baylor and West Virginia both ran all over them, for 281 and 203 yards, respectively, exploiting their inability to contain. The Sooners hope that interior defenders Jordan Kelley and Isaiah Coe can improve inside, spelled by six portal defensive line transfers of indeterminate ability. If you throw enough 300 pound guys at the problem, maybe one hits?

Oklahoma has upgraded their athleticism at linebacker, but their physicality remains in question. Particularly if opposing offenses don't concede that any Sooner on their defensive front is worthy of a double team.

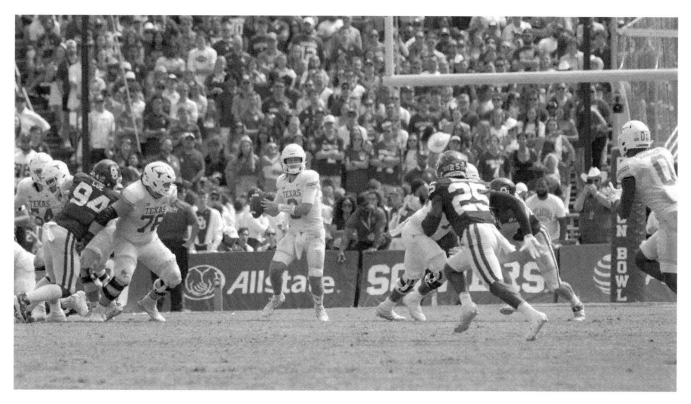

In the secondary, Oklahoma blew more than their share of coverages last year, but a smarter and more experienced group of safeties and an improved nickel should improve that. In fact, Billy Bowman and freshman Peyton Bowen are potential stars. Cornerback remains a potential neutral position, at least in the context of the ambitions that Venables has for this defense. Experienced veteran Woodi Washington returns (if you're looking for him in the Red River Shootout, Oklahoma started him at safety for that game) and the 5th year senior has about two dozen career starts. He has never bloomed into the dominant cornerback that was anticipated early in his career, but he's quality. Sophomore Gentry Williams will play opposite him and the former four star will be making his first start in the season opener, though he did get in 250 snaps last year as a freshman. Williams collapsed in March during a team drill and missed the rest of spring, but thankfully he made a full recovery and was cleared. Depth behind them is questionable and while Sooner fans said good riddance to former starting cornerback Jaden Davis after his transfer to Miami, they may sing a different tune if they encounter injuries.

HOUSTON COUGARS
October 21 | Houston, TX

BIG XII CONFERENCE
Dana Holgorsen | 5th season
2022 conference record 5-3

2022 RECORD	POINTS SCORED	POINTS ALLOWED
8-5	36.1	32.2
Not Ranked	#17 of 131	#112 of 131

RETURNING STARTERS
OFFENSE - 7 | DEFENSE - 4

Overview

With the additions of BYU and Houston, the Longhorns now have more cougars on their 2023 slate than a Longview Chili's happy hour. Houston has long been a major-minor job, one of the more coveted Group of 5 gigs that served to elevate coaching careers – see Art Briles to Baylor, Kevin Sumlin to Texas A&M, Tom Herman to Texas – while occasionally sticking high profile losses to Power 5 giants. Houston enthusiasts have long pointed to these upsets as proof that Houston belongs playing big boy football, ignoring the fact that playing a steady diet of Prairie View, Tulsa and Navy makes getting up for one big game a year pretty easy. Had Houston gone to the Big 12 in 2015 or 2021 with their best squads, they would have likely acquitted themselves well, but a program is as much defined by its troughs as it peaks. Right now, Houston is looking more peaked than peaky and in the sort of trough that says feeding time to their opponents.

Houston Cougar head coach Dana Holgorsen may find happy hour hunting grounds more generous than his inaugural season in the Big 12 as the 2023 Cougars will have to level up considerably without a handful of players who were the heart of the program over the last 2-3 years; specifically an offensive nucleus that made them a Top 25 national offense, the necessary component to overcome a defense that checked in around 90th.

Last year, the Cougars were supposed to win the AAC handily and were firmly listed in every preseason Top 25 poll (several cheeky national writers opined that they were the best team in Texas) but it never came to fruition. Some blame Cougar defensive coordinator Doug Belk's disappointing defense, others blame key injuries and the fact that Dana

Holgorsen's team was a coin flip every Saturday to look mentally engaged – the Cougars finished 124th in the country in penalty yards – but whatever the explanation, Houston was a low football IQ team that won eight games against a weak schedule despite themselves. Even Las Vegas struggled to understand the underachieving Cougs, who were 4-8 against the spread in the regular season.

The 2022 Cougars went 8-5 (5-3 in the AAC) against a strength of schedule firmly in the 60s. By contrast, no 2022 Big 12 team had an adjusted schedule strength outside of the Top 25. The shorthand of season record is how college fans discuss and evaluate success, but competition level is everything. By advanced metrics, Houston was the 58th best team in college football, roughly comparable to Troy, SMU and Western Kentucky. The Cougars were consistently inconsistent, getting smashed by Kansas (48-30) and SMU (77-63) by basketball scores; they beat Rice by a touchdown after trailing for a good portion of the game, lost to a Tulane team starting their 3rd string QB (he ended up with three passing touchdowns in that contest) and their bowl victory was a thoroughly unimpressive come-from-behind win over Louisiana-Lafayette.

Holgorsen is 27-20 after four years in Houston, including a 12-2 2021 campaign, but even that is a mirage. That 2021 nationally ranked Houston team was 41st in the country by advanced metrics, in part because they played a pathetic schedule against a slate of teams that went a collective 67-98 and featured only one ranked opponent. Their marquee win was a bowl victory over a 6-6 Auburn team and they recorded wins over juggernauts like 4-8 Rice, 4-7 Grambling, 4-8 Navy, 2-10 Tulane, 2-10 South Florida, 3-9 Temple and 1-11 UConn. Those seven teams combined for a 20-63 record. Outside of that season, the Cougars have been a sub .500 football team overall against weak competition. A more charitable interpretation is that Holgo had a rough start and that Houston has won 20 games in the last two seasons and is clearly on the upswing. Either narrative is pure spin, so let's deal with the realities of what Houston is in 2023.

The Cougars lost four players to the NFL draft, including three year starting QB Clayton Tune (who tossed 40 touchdowns in his last season and amassed over 11,000 career passing yards) and their greatest offensive weapon: wideout Tank Dell (1398 yards receiving, 17 touchdowns) who was drafted in the 3rd round. A quality experienced secondary was devastated by the Twin Horsemen of the Cougpocalypse – the draft and the portal – and once standout edge rusher Derek Parrish went down early in the season with injury, the Cougar pass rush was non-existent.

In 2023, the offense is likely to take a small step back against much better competition while the defense doesn't have many clear indicators of improvement. Like Memphis or Louisville, Houston can gather talent by osmosis, but a moderate rebuild while stepping up the competition level isn't advisable. The general inconsistency of the program last year also gives one considerable pause. The upside for this team looks like 6-6 while the floor looks something like 4-8, even with a non-conference schedule that includes Sam Houston State, UTSA and SMU. The Cougars will play 8 games in the city of Houston, including their first four of the season and six of their first seven overall. They need to win six of those games in H-Town to go bowling as road trips to Lubbock, Orlando, Manhattan and Waco will likely find them as substantial underdogs.

Strengths

Dana Holgorsen is always going to develop a capable passing game. Despite the massive loss of the diminutive Dell at wide receiver, the Cougars will still feature likely star Matthew Golden, up and comer USC transfer Joseph Manjack and steady Samuel Brown while adding two four star freshman receiver recruits in Jonah Wilson and Mikal Harrison-Pilot. Golden (38-584-7 touchdowns) is a screen game menace with long speed and should be their #1 pass catcher. He could easily have 75+ receptions this year. Manjack impressed in the Spring and this season promises a happy ending if he can catch more balls. Samuel Brown rounds out the key returnees and he was a steady contributor last year with 41 catches for 471 yards and 4 touchdowns. In addition to bringing in a great wide receiver recruiting class, Holgo snagged former Wyoming leading pass catcher Joshua Cobbs and Oklahoma State's Stephon Johnson from the portal. Houston has a quality room and this is a clear team strength. Good depth, talent and a strong diversity of skills are evident. A majority of Big 12 teams would trade their wide receiver room with the Cougars.

A smattering of players across the Cougar roster: center Jack Freeman, tackle Patrick Paul, New Mexico transfer safety Adari Houlcy and defensive end Nelson Caesar are all quality players. They will win plenty of individual matchups every Saturday. The problem is that they must be listed individually, because implying that the larger unit they belong to is also good or proven would be misleading. This is the fundamental problem with the Cougars. Their best players will be in NFL camps next year but alongside them they must start athletes who wouldn't make the two deep at high level FBS schools.

Weaknesses

The portal badly hurt Houston this offseason. The Cougars lost 1st team AAC guard Cam'Ron Johnson to Missouri, starting right tackle Lance Robinson to Louisville, starting safety Mannie "Get thee to a" Nunnery to Florida and star running back Alton McKaskill to Primetime's Colorado. Four clear starters, three of them among their best players. Houston did some work in the portal to patch their holes, nabbing West Virginia starting running back Tony Mathis, securing Sooner starting linebacker David Ugwoegbu (he will be moved to defensive end, his correct position), and filled out their two deep with a number of good performers from minor conferences – a total crapshoot there – but despite bringing in 20 portal athletes to build out their depth chart, some of those players are there to serve as camp bodies, not frontline talent.

Since 2022, the Cougars have lost ten offensive linemen and fired their offensive line coach (who was immediately hired by Missouri). Whether each individual player will be missed isn't really the point. Houston hasn't been hitting on their big man development and they are taking warm bodies to fill out their depth chart. Star left tackle Patrick Paul, center Jack Freeman and former Longhorn guard Tyler Johnson return with fellow ex-Longhorn Jaylen Garth expected to take over right tackle, but depth is currently so poor that the Cougar staff couldn't field ten linemen for a spring scrimmage. A couple of key injuries will effectively end their entire season.

The entire Houston secondary is composed of former transfers, three of them new to the campus this season. New Mexico sophomore safety Adari Hulcy proved to be the best player on the Lobo defense. He had an incredible 24 tackle game against Fresno State and looks to be a legitimate baller. Cornerback Isaiah Hamilton was a good performer at a losing Texas Southern program in the low level SWAC, nickel Latrell McCutchin is on his third school in three years (Oklahoma, USC, Houston) and senior safety Antonio Brooks is a career reserve forced into action by attrition and the portal. The last piece is cornerback Alex Hogan, who played two years at Texas Tech before playing three more at Houston while piecing together 8 starts over his entire career. The Cougars likely have a couple of players here – Hulcy and Hamilton are intriguing - but the balance of the secondary isn't very good.

Quarterback was a spring battle between Tech transfer Donovan Smith and Arkansas transfer Lucas Coley. Smith won. Smith would have been Texas Tech's 3rd string quarterback this year and while he is not without compelling physical traits, he hasn't evidenced consistent feel for the game and he can be a turnover factory. Texas fans overvalue Smith because he was the man behind center when Tech upset the Horns in Lubbock, but the truth is that his success in that game was aided by a poor defensive approach on key downs. He was benched two weeks later when opposing defensive coordinators didn't allow him to throw his few favored routes and removing Smith from the lineup is part of why Tech finished the season on a 4 game winning streak. Holgo is a fine a maximizer of quarterbacks and he will improve Smith significantly with the help of a quality group of pass catchers, but it's a fair bet that the passing game orchestra will be out of Tune.

BYU COUGARS
November 24 | Austin, TX

2022 RECORD	POINTS SCORED	POINTS ALLOWED
8-5	31.3	29.5
Not Ranked	#44 of 131	#97 of 131

BIG XII CONFERENCE
Kalani Sitake | 8th season
2022 conference record 0-0

RETURNING STARTERS
OFFENSE - 4 | DEFENSE - 7

Overview

BYU's program experienced a drop off with the departure of quarterback Zach Wilson, whose reign of terror over Cougar opponents and Salt Lake City soccer moms was as epic as the Wasatch mountains at sunrise. The 2023 Cougars will struggle to match his victories on and off the field, but the Cougs should be capable of succeeding in the Big 12 long term if they can fix their defense and capably exploit their new access to Texas recruiting markets. The Church Of Latter Day Saints is the fastest growing religion in Polynesia and that's a solid plus for Brigham Young U.

BYU head coach Kalani Sitake and Steve Sarkisian are former teammates, so the game in Austin will be a reunion of sorts. They can reminisce over big wins and their wild college days in Provo, like that time they drank sparkling waters and watched PG-13 movies until 10:30pm after beating Utah.

Kalani Sitake enters his eighth year in Provo and his career has been a study in patience. Sitake's first four years notched a 27-25 record, the program seemingly relegated to mediocrity. In 2020 and 2021 BYU broke out, going a combined 21-4 with two Top 20 finishes, featuring opportunistic defense and a terrific offense. An injury riddled 2022 campaign saw some regression from Sitake's apogee as the Cougs went 8-5, including a four game mid-season losing streak and a four game winning streak to close out the year. The Cougars will take a step up in schedule, highlighted by road trips to Arkansas, Kansas, TCU, Texas and a home stand against Oklahoma, but the Cougars landed a favorable slate overall (Cincy,

Oklahoma State, West Virginia, non-con snoozers against Sam Houston and Southern Utah) so a winning record is possible.

In 2022, the Cougars finished the season 24th in FBS offense by advanced statistics, but a bend-but-don't-break defensive philosophy yielded a 108th ranking. Combined with a spate of injuries, BYU's 8-5 2022 record looked very different from Texas' 8-5 mark, particularly given blowouts at the hands of Oregon and Liberty. The wisdom amongst BYU fans is that Sitake is at his best when he's recruiting, building culture and focusing on the big picture. BYU needs good coordinators that Sitake trusts so that he doesn't engage in micromanagement or focus on minutiae.

We must discuss the fact that LDS Superman Taysom Hill is not on the current BYU team so the pants pissing contingent amongst Longhorn fans can refocus on the relevant 2023 matchup and not the dying fumes of Mack Brown or doomed reign of Charlie Strong one decade past. As a reminder, in a 2013 home contest, Texas gave up 550 rushing yards to the Cougars. 349 of those yards in the first half. It was unpleasant. Please confidently take the under on that rushing number in 2023. Now that we have the unpleasantness out of the way...

As always, the X factor with any BYU football team will be 13 players returning from mission (who generally return older, lighter, with an exotic tropical illness – they all redshirt and have to rebuild their bodies), a whopping twenty two incoming portal transfers and their typically seasoned roster of super duper redshirted 25 year old grandparents. Adjusting to the big bodies in their new league will not pose a problem for them. Overall athleticism will. BYU should hang with the Big 12's best in most games until they are betrayed by deficits in quickness and big play ability. Until the Cougars get some more cats that can run, they will struggle to defend their mountain habitat.

Parting fun fact: when Texas and Oklahoma depart the conference, BYU's 63,470 seat stadium will be the largest in the Big 12. That same stadium in the 2024 SEC would be the 13th largest. The SEC will have five stadiums that seat over 100,000. The Big 12 will have nine that seat less than 60,000.

Strengths

BYU's starting quarterback is Kedon Slovis, a transfer from Pittsburgh (before that USC), who has seen his performance drop off markedly from his outstanding freshman year in

Los Angeles. In fairness, Slovis had a terrible offensive system for his skill set at Pitt and BYU offensive coordinator Aaron Roderick's offense and the personnel around him should suit his strengths better. Slovis is deeply experienced entering his 5th season as a starter and has compiled 68 career touchdown passes to 33 interceptions at 7.9 yards per passing attempt over his career, but when you back out the strong freshman year that accounted for 30 touchdowns and 9 interceptions at 8.9 yards per attempt, the reality of his last three years is very mediocre quarterback play. So why would he be listed as a strength? Because he may finally be in a situation that plays to his strengths: big catch radius receivers, ball control offense, not being asked to "create."

BYU skill players on offense are marginally better than is perceived though depth is poor. They have their usual mix of sure-handed, big bodied and "deceptively fast" wide receivers – Keanu Hill, Chase Roberts and Kody Epps – to plug into the mix. The 6-4, 210 pound Hill averaged nearly 16 yards per catch (36 catches, 572 yards) last year while scoring 7 touchdowns. Wiry Chase Roberts is also 6-4 and he chipped in 22 catches for 357 yards. Finally, Kody Epps is the "small quick guy" at 5-11, 185 and he scored 6 touchdowns on 39 balls. BYU doesn't have a true #1 receiver, but that means the ball goes to the best matchups or to the man that the coverage dicates. To round out the basketball team, tight end Isaac Rex goes 6-6, 260 and has 78 career catches with an incredible 21 touchdowns. He is a major red zone threat, finally healthy after a couple of injury plagued seasons. BYU isn't stocked with burners and receiver depth is poor if they have injuries, but the Cougs have quality options and their size and route running could pose a problem for smaller secondaries.

UNLV transfer Aidan Robbins goes 6-3, 230 and he was a 1,000+ yard rusher last year for an absolutely miserable Rebel offense. Robbins has good hands as well. He's a strong runner who will wear on smaller defenses, reminiscent of former Colorado running back Chris Brown. He is allergic to blocking, so putting him out on routes is preferable to turning him into a protector. Speaking of Colorado, backup running back Deion Smith is a refugee from Boulder. He's a decent player, but Robbins will be the bell cow. Don't be surprised if Robbins touches the ball 250+ times this season.

BYU did a nice job of shoring up their offensive line in the offseason after losing talent to the portal, turning a likely weakness into a passable unit. The centerpiece of the offensive line is left tackle Kingsley Suamataia, a 6-6, 315 pounder who is very high on NFL draft boards. Somehow they landed center Paul Maile from archrival Utah, who started for the

Utes last year and had a year left of graduate eligibility. They also lured right tackle Caleb Etienne from Oklahoma State. The 6-7, 330 pounder started 13 games in Stillwater, but Mike Gundy stated he transferred out because he got beat out. That's probably accurate as Etienne wasn't particularly good last year, despite very much looking the part. A change of scenery may do him good. He will line up next to 6-7, 330 pound guard Lisala Tai. Did I mention that BYU won't have much of an adjustment to the size of the athletes in a major football conference?

Weaknesses

In the offseason, Sitake fired his defensive coordinator and cleansed his S&C staff. Incoming defensive coordinator Jay Hill (previously the very successful former head coach at FCS Weber State) will adopt a different philosophy from his predecessor, but they'll need dramatic upgrades in defensive team speed to get out of last year's passive coverage philosophy. The Cougar secondary needs to level up athletically and will find themselves incapable of running with some of the top tier receiving groups in their new league. Hill will improve the unit and shift them to a 3-3-5 look, but Cougar upside likely rests on a re-tooled offense. Last year, opponents completed 67% of their pass attempts and collectively finished the season with a TD-INT ratio of 25-8. Hill wants to bring more pressure and tighter coverage and brought with him his FCS All-American cornerback Eddie Heckard to help achieve that. Now, he just needs three or four more.

The BYU defensive line got some new talent with two transfers from Boise State (Jackson Cravens and Isaiah Bagnah) and holdover defensive end Tyler Batty had seven sacks last year, but the entire unit is collectively FBS replacement level and it's hard to see a chance for a big leveling up. Their talent is sufficient if your goal is to qualify for a minor bowl, but the Cougars need more than adequacy from their front if they want to take pressure off of their defensive backs. Linebackers Ben Bywater and Max Tooley did their part, intercepting six balls between them last year (Tooley brought back two of them for touchdowns) and Bywater has led the Cougars in tackles for two years running. Unfortunately for BYU, an average front and a below average secondary can't be saved by quality linebackers.

KANSAS STATE WILDCATS

November 4 | Austin, TX

BIG XII CONFERENCE

Chris Klieman | 5th season
2022 conference record 7-2

2022 RECORD	POINTS SCORED	POINTS ALLOWED
10-4	32.3	21.9
#14 Final AP Rank	#37 of 131	#29 of 131

RETURNING STARTERS

OFFENSE - 7 | DEFENSE - 5

Overview

Ask a man on the street who won the Big 12 last year and they will tell you confidently that it was the TCU Horned Frogs. Of course, Kansas State won the Big 12 title, finally putting an end to the cardiac Frogs and their extraordinary ability to win tight games. A few weeks later, Georgia put an end to TCU's ability to win tight games in a different way. In their postseason Sugar Bowl, Kansas State was savaged 45-20 by an angry Alabama that played all of its draft eligible starters to prove a point about not being selected for the playoffs, but that was an anticlimax to an otherwise great year. Kansas State didn't quite have the Cinderella season that TCU did, but when they were 6-3 after road conference losses to Texas and TCU, they probably did not envision a 4-0 run and a Big 12 title, much less a 10 win season. Advanced metrics liked them even more than their 10-4 season record, ranking them as the 10th best squad in college football. Like TCU, they flourished when they started playing their backup quarterback and like the Frogs, they excelled when they paired a strong running game with an explosive deep passing game.

Similar to their purple brethren, they also lost many of their best football players to the NFL draft and graduation. The Wildcats return 12 starters in all, but only 5 on a denuded Wildcat defense.

Before talking strengths and weaknesses, a few words of praise for Chris Klieman. His 30-20 record at Kansas State is very solid, but how he has achieved it has been most impressive. Klieman won a Big 12 title with a team formed by the following recruiting rankings over the last 4 years per On3: 2019 – 67th, 2020 – 52nd, 2021 – 53rd, 2022 – 63rd. That's an average ranking of 59th in the country, on par with Cal and Colorado. How are those teams doing? Not great! A combined 5-19 last year. Interestingly, the Cats saw a recruiting bump in 2023 to the 30s and their 2024 class may also end up in that neighborhood if they can land a couple of four stars.

Of course Klieman can win with overachieving gritty kids ranked 59th, but how will he handle these primadonnas ranked 35th? Kansas State does a good job of developing talent, recruiting to their system and finding obscure FCS jewels in the portal, but when they play a high level team with more talent and comparable experience, the results will more often than not look a lot like the Sugar Bowl. That's not a knock on Kansas State, but a simple statement of athletic reality. The good news for the Wildcats is that those teams aren't very common and they can hang with anyone in the Big 12. This year's Cats will take a step down on defense, at least against higher order offenses. To mitigate that, Klieman will need to score points – which should not pose a problem – and control the clock at key junctures of the game. If Kansas State runs into a physical team that can thwart their standard downs run game and chain-moving play action tosses to the tight end and running backs, they may find their defense uncomfortably exposed.

Strengths

Want to know one reason why Kansas State punches above their weight? Playing 23 and 24 year olds against 20 year olds. The Wildcats return their entire offensive line and most of them have been shaving for a while. A couple of them are AARP members.

Left guard Cooper Beebe is a 1st team All-American who graded out with 5 missed blocks in 940 snaps last year. The 6-4, 330 pounder is surprisingly mobile as a puller and a merciless road grader on inside runs. The 5th year senior has 35 career starts. Left tackle 6-5, 330 pound KT Leveston returns for his 6th year and is proof of the power of incremental improvement, playing at replacement level for most of his career in spot starts until breaking out with 14 starts and 909 snaps in 2022 and positioning himself as a likely low round NFL Draft pick. Center Hayden Gillum is a 6th year player as well. Right guard Hadley Panzer is the rare non-redshirted Wildcat lineman, which means the junior must be pretty solid. Big 6-6, 310 pound right tackle Christian Duffie rounds out the unit and yes, of course, he's also a 6th year player. All three of them played 900+ snaps last year. As if that wasn't enough, Kansas State will return their entire three deep, including former starting guard

Taylor Poitier, who injured his knee in the opener, but has made a full recovery. The Wildcats start a great player, a good player and three experienced just above replacement level players. Their cohesion is generally excellent and while they are a fine run blocking unit, they can be uneven in pass protection, grading out last season as below average in pressures allowed.

The brightest spot on the Wildcat defense is their linebackers. Tackling machine Austin Moore, 245 pound enforcer Daniel Green and newcomer Desmond Purnell anchor the middle of the Wildcat 3-3-5. The 220 pound Moore is their leading tackler and he's terrific when the Cats can keep him clean. The former walk on is very instinctive. The 6th year Green brings physicality and punch inside to go with 27 career starts. Despite his size, he's sneaky good in coverage and nabbed two interceptions last year to go with his 9.5 career sacks as a blitzer. Purnell is the newcomer and he plays as a hybrid space linebacker so common in the Big 12. The 5-11, 220 pound athlete can turn and run with tight ends and isn't out of place in coverage. This is the strength of the Wildcat defense.

Will Howard was a bad quarterback until he wasn't. Before last year, the giant 6-5, 245 pound dual threat quarterback had combined for ten starts and several relief efforts over two years compiling a passing profile of 223-120-1510 yards with 9 touchdowns and 11 interceptions. He completed only 54% of his passes and averaged less than 7 yards per completion. The NFL wasn't knocking down his door and his own head coach was not impressed, choosing former Husker Adrian Martinez to be the man in Manhattan. Martinez floundered as a passer and Howard excelled, stealing the job and leading the Cats to title glory while hitting 60% of his passes and a succession of clutch deep balls while throwing 15 touchdowns, only 4 interceptions and compiling 1633 passing yards at over 8.2 yards per attempt. Thus conclusively proving that Chris Klieman is a bad coach who can't evaluate his own team. Just kidding.

Though always a capable runner, Howard didn't run the ball much last year, saving on some aches and pains that doubtlessly improved his accuracy. Howard is excellent at buying time in the pocket (which he had to do frequently) with his feet and size and his off schedule ability to improvise is impressive. With Howard in the lineup, Kansas State averaged 8 points per game more on offense. You'll be hard pressed to find a team more excited to return a quarterback with a career 7-9 record as a starter.

H-back Ben Sinnott's stat line of 31 catches, 447 yards and 4 touchdowns last year was fine, but it somehow understates the impact that Sinnott seemed to have in every big game. A soft-handed pass catcher in the seam and a capable blocker, Sinnott should be expected to catch 50+ balls this year as the Kansas State Wildcat receiving corps will be league average, scrambling to find replacements for #1 target Malik Knowles and route runner par excellence Kade Warner. Speedy Phillip Brooks does return, but the 5-8 170 pound pass catcher can't provide the big target that Knowles and Warner did. Kansas State should be OK here, but Sinnott will shoulder a big portion of the passing load.

It's sacrilege to list running back as a team strength with the departure of the extraordinary Deuce Vaughn and his nearly 2,000 yards from scrimmage, but Kansas State will have a high level running back room. 210 pound DJ Giddens was great as a freshman spelling Deuce. He had 89 carries for 519 yards and 6 touchdowns at 5.8 yards per carry. He also added 8 catches for 98 yards. He was a bright spot against Alabama in the Sugar Bowl, ripping off a 30 yard run and catching a 36 yard pass. He totaled over 100 yards from scrimmage in their loss. Joining him is fleet-footed Treshaun Ward from Florida State. Ward was splitting running back duties with high level runner Trey Benson and his transfer was a surprise given that he had 94 carries for 628 yards and 7 touchdowns rushing at 6.7 yards per carry, which led the ACC in terms of explosiveness. The 190 pound runner looked great scoring two touchdowns on Oklahoma in the Cheez-It Bowl and he turned blocking lemons into lemonade with an elusive style. He has 28 career catches, so he can also catch the ball out of the backfield. The falloff behind these two is steep, but a 50/50 rotation should keep them both fresh.

Weaknesses

The idea that the Kansas State defense will simply shrug off the departure of multiple high round NFL draft picks and several outstanding role players is ambitious optimism. The Cats lost all of their defensive backs except for Kobe Savage. The losses include 2nd round draft pick press corner Julius Brents, quality cornerback Ekow Boye-Doe and their speediest safety, NFL draftee Josh Hayes. Cornerback will be a major concern though Klieman will try to get by with the solid Jacob Parrish (played 300+ snaps last year) and the less than solid former JUCO Jordan Wright or JUCO Will Lee. They love sophomore safety VJ Payne, who started four games last year. He starred for a high school powerhouse in Buford, GA, but slipped through the SEC recruiting cracks to end up in Manhattan. Intriguing player. The other safety spot will feature FCS transfer Marques Sigle from North Dakota State. Klieman has a great record with these under-the-radar additions, but Sigle was just a rotation player there. Finally, you will see Kobe Savage on multiple preseason All Big 12 teams. He's fine but not a Top 5 safety in the league. This group takes a step down.

Felix Anuduke-Uzomah's loss will be felt (8.5 sacks, 2 forced fumbles) on the edge, but don't forget about outstanding run plugging nose tackle Eli Huggins. Huggins got better every year in Manhattan and finished his senior year as the highest graded defensive player on the team. Khalid Duke will hold down one end spot. He's been adequate, though if you saw him collect 3 sacks against Texas Tech, you probably thought he was Von Miller. He didn't have another sack the entire season. Brendan Mott (6 sacks last year) and Nate Matlack should be fine at the other edge. The interior defensive line is questionable and Kansas State badly lacks front line size overall. Throw in a smallish linebacker group and it can get dicey. It won't necessarily bite them against most teams, but Texas mauled them in the trenches last year for 6.6 yards per carry and 269 yards rushing. That's replicable again. Given a questionable secondary and an uneven defensive line, not even good linebacker play can elevate this defense to 2022 levels.

TCU HORNED FROGS
November 11 | Fort Worth, TX

2022 RECORD	POINTS SCORED	POINTS ALLOWED
13-2	38.8	29
#2 Final AP Rank	#9 of 131	#91 of 131

BIG XII CONFERENCE
Sonny Dykes | 2nd season
2022 conference record 9-0

RETURNING STARTERS
OFFENSE - 3 | DEFENSE - 8

Overview

The TCU Horned Frogs completed an improbable and unexpected playoff run last year with a 13-2 record and a #2 postseason ranking in the final coaches poll, but suffered a brutal mauling in the national title game at the hands of the Georgia Bulldogs. That 65-7 destruction by the Bulldogs overshadowed an improbable run which featured harrowing wins over Michigan, Texas, Baylor, Kansas and Oklahoma State all by a score or less complemented by more satisfying obliterations of Oklahoma and Iowa State.

No team wants to be humiliated on the biggest stage or lose 2 of their last 3 after a 12-0 start, but overall the Frogs had an incredible year; even if deeper dives into the metrics (and film room) leaves you wondering how the 12th ranked team in the nation by advanced statistics played for all of the marbles.

A close loss to Kansas State in the Big 12 title game wasn't enough to keep them out of the playoffs, but it did suggest that TCU's penchant for close wins was as reliant on the ball bouncing a certain way in tight contests as a talented senior laden football team that perfected a style of play that kept catching their opponents off guard. Deeply experienced talent at key positions influenced TCU's favorable narrow margins in close games, but what happens to clutchness and gritty winnerness when the talented seniors depart?

Most national and regional media see TCU taking a modest step back in 2023, but they all temper that prediction with an insistence that TCU will remain a Top 15 team and a Big 12 title contender. After all, why would a team get significantly worse due to something as inconsequential as losing all of their best players? ESPN had TCU at #12 in its too early 2023 predictions. Athlon has them at #15. USA Today has them ranked at #16. The Horned Frogs – boasting a 40-34 record (26-28 in Big 12 play) over the six years prior to 2022 – are just reloading instead of rebuilding in the eyes of the national media. In a culture where full news cycles last as long as a TikTok video, perhaps one can be forgiven for thinking the Horned Frogs are a blue (purple) blood that simply reloads.

They are not. The polls reveal a fundamental misunderstanding of what drove TCU's 2022 success and a failure to see how the loss of most of their key drivers will result in a dramatically different football team.

TCU lost the following from their 2022 squad:

QB Max Duggan (Big 12 OPOY, led league in passing efficiency, #3 team rusher, 43 career starts, 7th round NFL)

WR Quentin Johnston (1st team All Big 12, 1069 yards receiving, 1st round NFL)

RB Kendre Miller (1st team All Big 12, 1399 yards rushing, 6.2 yards per carry, 3rd round NFL)

OG Steve Avila (1st team All Big 12 OG, 1st team All America, 35 career starts, 2nd round NFL)

C Alan Ali (1st team All Big 12 C, 56 career starts!)

DL Dylan Horton (led team in sacks with 10, 14.5 tfl tied for team lead, 4th round NFL)

CB Tre Hodges Tomlinson (1st team All Big 12, 1st team All America, 38 career starts, 6th round NFL)

LB Dee Winters (1st team All Big 12, 2nd on team with 7.5 sacks, 14.5 tfl tied for team lead, 6th round NFL)

WR Taye Barber (#2 pass catcher, 52 career starts)

WR Derius Davis (Big 12 Special Teams POY, 1st team All America KR, #3 pass catcher, 40 career starts, 4th round NFL)

RB Emari Demarcado (#2 RB, 681 yards rushing, 5.6 yards per carry)

Eight of those departed players were drafted to the NFL and five of them went in the first 125 picks. By pure player power ranking, TCU loses seven of their eight best players and eleven of their best sixteen overall. Beyond the loss of multiple NFL studs, they lose a total aggregation of experience rarely seen in college football. Losing multiple three and four year starters with between 35-56 career starts has consequences.

TCU hit the transfer portal and nabbed some former big name recruits without a lot of production and some will come through for them, but half of their haul for key starting spots are athletes from places like Stephen F Austin, Jackson State and a grab bag of junior colleges. Hidden gems can be found, but obvious gems are vastly preferable. To test this theory, hand your wife a metal detector on a beach and tell her to look for ten hours or offer to make a trip to Tiffany and see which one she is more enthusiastic about.

Finally, a warning to those who can't let a season unfold before making pronouncements (judging from this preview, I can't either). TCU's 2023 season schedule begins with Colorado, Nicholls State, SMU, Houston and West Virginia. Not a murderer's row, is it? The Frogs may well be sitting pretty at 5-0 with a lofty national ranking as the sports pablum factory cranks out Sonny Dykes, Just A Winner content, but September optimism will give way to mid-October and November realism when they play conference opponents who can fog a mirror. TCU's schedule is incredibly favorable overall and this will artificially buoy their win total, but the Frogs will start falling with the leaves in November.

Strengths

TCU may have the best overall secondary in the Big 12. Losing eternal starter Trevius Hodges-Tomlinson at cornerback is a loss, but the secondary is deep, experienced and has quality that forces athletes who would be starters on most other campuses into backup and rotational roles. Cornerback Josh Newton was 1st Team All Big 12 last year and led the Frogs in pass breakups. He has 24 career starts and he's a perfect blend of size and speed for the position. Fourth year nickel Bud Clark was an unexpected revelation and the rangy 6-2, 190 pound playmaker led the Frogs with five interceptions, including a brilliant pick six against Michigan. Super senior strong safety Mark Perry was TCU's second leading tackler and he has surprising straight line speed at 215 pounds. He's average in coverage, but he can bring the wood. Senior Millard Bradford has 20 career starts at free safety and is the forgotten man of the TCU secondary, but a stalwart nonetheless. They bring in new cornerback Avery Helm from Florida, who Frog coaches consider a high level press man defender that wasn't properly utilized in Gainesville. Florida fans beg to differ and believe he fled as his playing time rightfully dwindled. If Helm fails, they have #2 JUCO cornerback prospect Channing Canada and the multipurpose Abe Camara, who had 54 tackles last year as a part-time starter and heavy rotation guy. Only Texas has comparable quality and depth but the Frogs are more battle tested.

The Toad defense returns eight starters and has a much better chance of showing re-silience than their offense despite losing their three most disruptive defenders to the NFL Draft. Sophomore nose tackle Damonic Williams is an outstanding youngster who shined as a true freshman, linebacker Jamoi Hodge has perfected the art of targeting starting quarterbacks – understanding the arbitrage that a one game suspension is well worth play-ing against the other team's second team passer – and Johnny Hodges is a really good meat and potatoes linebacker. They'll need that secondary and linebacker corps to play at an extremely high level to offset a lack of pass rush (the departed Winters and Horton were responsible for 17.5 of their sacks) and compensate for the uneven bunch of role players that round out their defensive front. Depth matters up front and the Frogs don't have it.

TCU should be commended for their work in the portal to replace all of their departed skill players. They bring in Alabama's unproven but talented Jojo Earle to play the slot, grabbed rock steady JP Richardson from Oklahoma State to serve as their possession receiver (49 catches, 503 yards for the Cowboys in 2022) and took a shot in the dark on former elite recruit and head case Dylan Wright from Minnesota (via Texas A&M) who grabbed 35 balls over two seasons. They'll join big 6-5, 215 pound X receiver Savion Williams, who had 29 catches last year for 392 yards and 4 touchdowns. Williams is great at contested catches, an important trait given that he can't separate. Running back Trey Sanders was shown the door at Alabama and will try to reinvigorate his career in Ft Worth. He will have to beat out the underappreciated Emani Bailey first. TCU takes a step down in skill talent across the board, but without their offseason work, TCU's offensive decline would have been disastrous.

Weaknesses

Before last year, 2020 was the last time that TCU had a meaningful haul of NFL draft picks (with four Frogs going in the first 3 rounds, five drafted overall). After that draft, the Frogs went from a winning conference record to a 3-6 in-league debacle that led to the departure of their all-time winningest coach. Offensively, they return only 33% of their production, which ranks 130th in all of FBS. They'll also turn the offense over to a new quarterback: the talented, but slightly built Chandler Morris. Morris will be hard pressed to match Duggan's efficient turnover free big play production via leg and arm.

They lost an entire starting receiving corps that was the most experienced in college football. They also trade out excellent offensive coordinator Garrett Riley for a pretty good Kendal Briles, who will bring a different version of the spread that requires significant QB run components in order for it to maximize. Briles wants to run the ball and take deep shots, but the sooner he adapts the offense to Chandler Morris' actual skill set of quick recognition and accuracy in the intermediate game, the better TCU will be. A fair number of TCU fans deeply despise Baylor and the Briles legacy, so Dykes may regret such a tone deaf hire if the Briles offense doesn't pan out. Obviously, Dykes is invulnerable right now after last year's run, but if TCU fails with Briles on their staff, Sonny will burn a lot of goodwill.

TCU's outstanding running game loses two very good ball carriers and its two best blockers. The offensive line has the potential to be alright - particularly if Jackson State transfer Willis Patrick pans out at guard - but they will sorely miss big Steve Avila's run blocking and center Alan Ali's leadership, experience (50+ career starts) and coordination at center. Avila and

Ali were largely responsible for TCU's A-level A-gap run game and Avila was probably the most physically dominant run blocking lineman in the conference. Purple optimists point to returning tackles Andrew Coker and Brandon Coleman as a crucial base for 2023 continuity, but Coker is Diet Coke as a pass protector and while Coleman is good, depth behind each is non-existent.

IOWA STATE CYCLONES

November 18 | Ames, IA

2022 RECORD	POINTS SCORED	POINTS ALLOWED
4-8	20.2	20.2
Not Ranked	#114 of 131	#18 of 131

BIG XII CONFERENCE

Matt Campbell | 8th season
2022 conference record 1-8

RETURNING STARTERS

OFFENSE - 9 | DEFENSE - 7

Overview

Since their breakout 9-3 record in 2020, Iowa State has gone 11-14 and is a disappointing 6-12 in conference play. That's not how it was supposed to go for a program that had turned the corner with national rankings and serious talk of Big 12 titles. 2021's "Best Team In School History" fizzled to 7-6 and the 2022 blue collar get-back-to-Cyclone-football bunch went 4-8 and 1-8 in conference play, losing six games by a touchdown or less. Texas was only a Xavier Worthy jerk route touchdown and an Anthony Cook forced fumble away from getting upset in Austin, narrowly edging them 24-21. That 4-8 mark was the first losing season for Iowa State since 2016, One bright spot is that they did beat rival Iowa in a 10-7 snoozer to win a Costco Membership (OK, it's the Cy-Hawk Trophy) and their defense was statistically the best unit in the Big 12. Also, most college fans would rather watch tortoises hump than witness Iowa State play offense.

It is amusing to read some Cyclone fans musing over whether it's time to part ways with a winning coach given that they haven't had a coach with a winning record since Earle Bruce went 36-32 between 1973-1978, but Campbell created expectations that he will have to meet. Iowa State fans grumbling about Matt Campbell need to stop guzzling government subsidized ethanol. Iowa State was 8-28 the three years before Matt Campbell arrived on campus and he is solely responsible for creating the expectations by which they judge him. Unfortunately, Campbell also exhibited a bit of hubris, believing that he could turn Iowa State into a perennial winner that didn't have to honor the traditional cycles of a Big 12 developmental program. Wrong. They are in a down cycle and Campbell didn't get the memo that he was already supposed to have jumped ship for a better job by now. Did I mention that Matt Campbell doesn't have an agent? If he had one, this would have been explained to him.

This offseason, Campbell cleaned house on his coaching staff. When the pink slips started flying around Ames, defensive coordinator Jon Heacock probably wasn't too concerned. He may have been concerned by the fact that Campbell executed the dreaded internal promotion at offensive coordinator, elevating 32 year old wide receivers coach Nathan Scheelhaase to the booth; performed the obligatory firing of the S&C coach (we just need to get stronger, wait, no, we need to get more flexible, wait, no we need to get faster, wait, no, we need to get stronger... repeat) and brought in new offensive line coach Ryan Clanton from Northern Iowa. Clanton has an excellent reputation as a rising star offensive line coach and the staff overhaul brings reinvigorating ideas to the offense at every position. There is no question that Iowa State's stale offense needed revamping, but the truth is that Campbell's preferences and mandates are what created it.

Iowa State is currently a popular pick to "surprise" and you will hear analysts muse that "Matt Campbell hasn't forgotten how to coach" but talk is cheap and the Cyclones fail several key litmus tests that signal a big turnaround. The notion that they were a few plays away from 6-6 or 8-4 last year is 100% accurate. They were also a play away from 3-9. It also obfuscates the fact that they were oh so close to being a winning team due to some of their best players who don't wear cardinal and gold anymore. Returning sixteen starters is great for continuity, but returning all of the JAGS who can't execute an inside zone block doesn't carry much weight. Though given the firing of their S&C coach, perhaps no one on their team can carry enough weight.

Strengths

Jon Heacock, you splendid bastard, you did it again! The veteran defensive coordinator crafted yet another winning defense with some talent, some coaching and a lot of continuity. Iowa State's defensive secret is that they don't start bad football players, which sounds easy enough, but creating roles for what would be average or possibly bad players in other schemes that makes them play good football in Heacock's scheme isn't easy at all. Sprinkle in a couple of NFL draft picks and you've got another Big 12 leading defense. Heacock is comfortable in his own skin and while every other defensive coordinator drops

wrestling promos about aggression, blitzing more and attacking, Heacock shrugs, drops eight defenders and watches offenses fail. Heacock isn't perfect, but when you adjust for their talent, he is quite impressive. The Cyclones lost the dynamism of 1st round edge Will McDonald and the hard-hitting experience of safety Anthony Johnson to the NFL draft along with some very key role players like defensive end MJ Anderson and linebacker O'Rien Vance, but the defense is hardly bereft. They could take a moderate step down, but they will still play good ball. As long as they have Heacock calling the shots, Iowa State will be in most ballgames.

Iowa State has a good secondary, led by cornerbacks TJ Tampa and Myles Purchase. TJ Tampa sounds like a bad drive time radio host, but Tampa is a long corner with great ball skills from – you guessed it – Florida. They say breaking up is hard to do, but Tampa had nine of them last year. Myles Purchase is a solid partner in the corner duo and my fourth favorite Purchase after the Gadsden Purchase of 1853, the Louisiana Purchase of

1803 and a Roomba. 6-2, 210 pound safety Beau Freyler led the defense with 3 picks last year and in his team picture he's wearing a headband, which makes him look like a pervy aerobics instructor. He was second on the team in tackles and he's a good deep zone defender. In the same vein, Malik Verdon brings length on the back end at 6-4, 215, but thankfully, no headband. Sophomore nickel Jeremiah Cooper played a lot last year, so no concerns about inexperience there. The Cyclones have great length and good corners. Good unit.

Weaknesses

You wouldn't know that Hunter Dekkers was a weakness last year given how he torched the Horns in Austin going 25 of 36 for 329 yards with two touchdowns and an interception while adding another 30 yards rushing. Leave it to Pete Kwiatkowski's defensive scheme to struggle against Hunter Dekkers and Donovan Smith and contain Bryce Young, Max Duggan and Michael Penix. Hunter left more upper Dekkers for his own offense than for opponents, which explains no bowl. Dekkers threw 14 costly interceptions to offset his 3,000+ yards at a poor 6.7 yards per attempt, but in Dekkers' defense, he had 26 drops from his receiving corps, 14 interceptions at over 500 passing attempts is actually less than 3% and the offense had absolutely no running game. In truth, he can throw a pretty nice ball. So Dekkers may not be as bad as the numbers suggest, but he is certainly representative of the failures of the Cyclone offense overall. He may also represent a lapse in Iowa State's Self-Proclaimed 5 Star Culture. While still all very hush-hush, there are credible reports that several Iowa State athletes – possibly to include Dekkers – were involved in placing wagers on sports. That's naughty and the NCAA may have a say in this matter, as well as the FBI, INTERPOL and the local Kiwanis Club. If he misses games, Iowa State will likely start 6-7 true freshman JJ Kohl or redshirt freshman Rocco Becht.

The Iowa State running game was execrable last year. They averaged a miserable 108 yards per game at 3.3 yards per carry. Blame a running back room of mediocrities and terrible offensive line push, but the Cyclones schemes were more basic than TJ Maxx. They failed to eclipse 100 yards rushing against six Big 12 opponents, never once topped 200 rushing yards and were held to 26 rushing yards by Kansas. Eleven random readers of this preview could get 26 yards against Kansas. Though they have upgraded their offensive line coach, returning most of the players who were responsible for last year's run game travesty is not positive news.

The remarkable Xavier Hutchinson is off to the NFL and few receivers have done more surrounded by so little. Hutchinson caught 107 balls for 1171 yards as a senior and his 162 passing targets made up a significant focus of the Iowa State passing attack. They do return Jaylin Noel and Dimitri Stanley and they combined for 93 catches last year. They have some positive attributes, but their primary weakness has been football. They add 6-3, 215 pound Jayden Higgins from Eastern Kentucky to fill the Hutchinson role and he's at least directional Kentucky good. Iowa State's receivers will improve individually, but the void of Hutchinson's loss will be apparent and the upside of this unit is firmly around league average. Fortunately, this is Iowa State and they always have a 6-6 tight end running around somewhere and this time it's DeShawn "Happy" Hanika. He's got more wingspan than a menorah and had 17 catches last year. Solid player. His backup is named Stevo Klotz. He's likely irrelevant to their offensive production, but it's good to know there's a guy named Stevo Klotz out there.

Generally, good football coaches don't have awful special teams, but Iowa State was ranked 128th last year. The year before, they were 101st. In 2020? 90th. This is not trending the right way. If you want to find a sneaky reason that the Cyclones have lost of their conference games over the last two years, Iowa State kickers connected on only 56% of field goal attempts last year, including Jace Gilbert's three misses between 38-45 yards against Kansas in a 3 point loss. Iowa State returners muffed multiple punts, coverage men committed dumb personal fouls and Iowa State's returners ran like they were mired in molasses. Campbell hired a new special teams coach as part of his revamp, but it's clear that Iowa State has either devoted insufficient time and attention to the special teams units, have a slow roster behind the front line starters, or just can't find a kicker. Some combination of all three are likely.

TEXAS TECH RED RAIDERS

November 24 | Austin, TX

2022 RECORD	POINTS SCORED	POINTS ALLOWED
8-5	34.2	29.2
Not Ranked	#27 of 131	#93 of 131

BIG XII CONFERENCE

Joey McGuire | 2nd season
2022 conference record 5-4

RETURNING STARTERS

OFFENSE - 8 | DEFENSE - 6

Overview

Joey McGuire's 2022 debut as Texas Tech's head football coach marked the 5th leader of that program since Adam James started snapping selfies in a storage shed.

Generally, that kind of turnover isn't associated with winning. Joey McGuire's 5-4 Big 12 record was the first winning conference mark in Lubbock since Mike Leach's last year in Lubbock. Between 2010-2021, the Raiders were an execrable 36-71 in conference play, posting zero winning tallies in any year of conference action. They were consistent, predictable losers despite having multiple NFL quarterbacks pass through their campus during that time period. These guys even sucked with Patrick Mahomes!

For a program that had grown accustomed to college football's comfortable upper middle class under Mike Leach (84-43, a 66% winning percentage, Top 25 finishes in 5 of his last 6 seasons), the fall from grace left their fan psyche bleaker than a Muleshoe mud storm. Beyond the decade of winning that Leach brought, Texas Tech football under Mike Leach – may he rest in peace – was a lot of fun and the Raiders became a quirky fan favorite with national interest. Ever since Texas Tech administrators effectively framed Leach in order to fire him, the Llano Estacado has been in a fun drought. Waiting for Leach to pass before offering to induct him posthumously into the Texas Tech Hall of Fame was a feeble attempt at repentance; pathetically bush league would be a kind description of that insincere gesture.

Anway, last year, the drought finally broke.

Back in 2022, the preview favorably opined that Texas Tech's hire of Joey McGuire was tantamount to hiring their Jeff Traylor and that McGuire's innovative staff hires proved that he "got it." Texas Tech finally found a coach. That prediction proved out nicely in the 2022 season.

McGuire was a longtime, well-regarded Texas high school football coach from Cedar Hill with a scant five years of position coaching at the college level. From a conventional re-sume standpoint, he had no business being hired. From a trait standpoint, Tech made a compelling selection. McGuire had the traits to successfully lead a college program. What he lacked was credentials. Previous credential hires Tommy Tuberville (veteran proven winner!) and Matt Wells (up and comer!) didn't work out and young guru Kliff Kingsbury bottomed out despite his offensive numbers. It was time to try something different. Could McGuire prove that good coaching is good coaching no matter the level? What if that coach marries old fashioned red ass motivation with a cutting edge understanding of game-winning analytics?

The returns are still early, but so far, so good.

Last year, Texas Tech went 8-5, beat both Texas and Oklahoma, crushed Ole Miss in a bowl game and finished the year with a 4-0 run that left Red Raider fans positively giddy. That they did it with a team that was not very talented made it all the more improbable. The Red Raiders were overachieving underdogs and they did it in a novel way: by pairing some old school Texas high school football cussedness with the guts and analytical sophistication to understand that attacking on 4th down is a cheat code for winning football games. If you compare Tech's season numbers to their projected win expectation, they finished a full two games ahead of expectation. That was not luck. Texas Tech stole games from better teams unprepared to deal with their game theory supported – but dumb media critiqued – 4th down aggression.

While commenters criticized Tech's 4th down gimmickry with the predictable characteriza-tions: "teenager playing Madden energy", "unsound football" and "risky exposure of their defense", the Red Raiders rode 4th down aggression and mental toughness to their best season in a dozen years.

Their macro statistical profile was gross. Texas Tech gave up more yards per play than they gained (5.5 vs. 5.9), surrendered sacks in droves (41), finished 99th in the country in turnover margin and three Raider quarterbacks combined to throw 18 interceptions despite

a dink and dunk offensive passing system that had little ability to push the ball downfield. The defense surrendered a lot of big plays and Tech spent most of the year alternating between replacing an injured starter or benching a non-performer at quarterback. They failed many statistical measures that predict season success. They simply did not fit the profile of a winning football team. What happened?

In key individual games, Texas Tech absolutely owned 4th down. On offense and defense. Tech went for it on 4th down more than any team in the country – 52 times – and converted 33 of those attempts into a new set of downs or points. That robust 63.5% conversion rate and a willingness to go for it so often had a material impact on game outcomes. The impact of their 4th down strategy wasn't just felt on the money down itself, which is substantial in determining drive and scoring success, but also in how defenses called their 3rd down defense, experienced psychological deflation at their inability get off of the field and, in some games, endured never-ending Raider drives while their offense sat ice cold on the sideline.

This wasn't just about going for it on 4th down. It's about an approach to football. A punt is a controlled turnover. A coach who punts on 4th and 4 on the opponent 41 yard line is not being conservative. He has a severe intellectual or testicular deficit. A 4th down stop or conversion improves material chances of winning, but it also can impact the psychology of the opponent. Analysts or coaches who refuse to consider this simply don't see the game as it is. Against Texas, the Raiders converted 6 of 8 on 4th down. There's no chance they win the game without that atypical aggression and had they gone 0-3 on their first three attempts, there never would have been eight total attempts.

Lane Kiffin's Ole Miss came into the Texas Bowl seemingly prepared and determined to match Tech's 4th down aggression and the two teams went for it a combined nine times in the 1st half alone. The team that had owned 4th down all year converted 75% of their 4th down attempts. The Rebels were 1 of 5. Halftime score? Tech- 27, Ole Miss- 7.

This wasn't just about the willingness to go for it. Defending 4th down is also crucial. Red Raider opponents went for it on 4th down a robust 32 times during the year. They converted only 34% of those attempts, making Tech the 8th best 4th down defense in college football. Texas Tech wasn't even a Top 60 defense on the other three downs!

How? Tech was unpredictable and assertive, knowing that most offenses have a limited menu of 4th down options. Tech's defense rarely honored football conventions on key downs. 4th and short around midfield? Load the box and dare a long throw into single coverage. Most offensive coaches blink and will run it into a stunting linebacker. 4th and medium? Tech would run an exotic look and force the quarterback to solve novelty. 4th down pressure and a flustered quarterback yielded bad plays. Meanwhile, Tech's offense, which converted a mediocre 37% on 3rd down performed 26 percentage points better on 4th down. No team in college football had a wider positive spread in 4th down vs regular down performance on both sides of the ball than the Raiders. By refusing to play the game as dictated by football tradition, they played the real game by the actual numbers with the appropriate asymmetrical tactics.

The best swordsman doesn't fear the 15th best swordsman. He fears an ordinary man with a crossbow who doesn't agree that it's a sword fight.

Given time and reflection, most opponents adjust to novel approaches and should better prepare their teams psychologically and tactically. Joey McGuire's next evolution must be progressing middling units into winning more on regular downs while finding more cheat codes in the game that are hidden in plain sight.

Strengths

Texas Tech returns 14 starters, 8 of them on offense. 18 of their starters this year are super seniors and some of them have been around for as many as seven years. This is a deeply veteran team and if you're a student of Big 12 developmental cycles, Tech is very much at the top of one of theirs. 2024 Texas Tech returning only 4 starters will be pretty interesting, but the focus is on 2023.

Last year, offensive coordinator Zach Kittley struggled to establish an offensive identity, scraping together whatever he thought might move the ball, but another year in the system should clarify roles and expectations. Now the coaching staff has a much better idea of who can actually be trusted to execute Kittley's high volume, fastbreak offense.

The Red Raiders will attack defenses with a deep receiving corps, blistering pace and volume of opportunity. Slot Myles Price returns (51-513) to provide stability and even more 4th down conversions in the middle of the field. Last year, 6-5 sophomore Jerand Bradley grew into the team's #1 option (51-744-6 touchdowns) outside and heralded FCS transfer Drae McCray from Austin Peay brings 1,888 yards receiving and 17 touchdowns over 22 games and a rep for shaking defenders after the catch. Heavy in the rotation will be 6-4 215 pound Loic Fouonji (34 catches last year), 6-4 220 pound JJ Sparkman (14 catches) and 6th year senior Xavier White, a former running back with 751 career rushing yards who had 45 catches last year as a full-time receiver. Texas Tech's receiver room goes six deep with solid options and Kittley will throw them at defenses in waves, half of the unit wearing down opponents with their size and physicality, the other half of the unit forcing the defense to chase speed laterally and vertically all over the field. Running this corps at breakneck pace, with every player going full speed on every play in hockey line shifts, is a clever approach for a volume offense and, over time, most secondaries will begin to degrade and miss tackles from simple exhaustion.

Former Oregon Duck quarterback Tyler Shough is cemented as the Red Raider starter after a strong finish to the season and a winning performance in the bowl game against Ole Miss. The 6-5, 230 pound signal caller from Chandler, AZ has a big arm and an easy release and he can run when needed (he had 25 carries for 111 yards and two touchdowns in their bowl win). Shough has become the offensive conduit that Kittley needs and has embraced Don't Think, Just Do pre-snap reads and quick throws that Kittley's offense thrives on. Tyler is 12-4 as a college starter and 8-1 at Texas Tech in games that he started and finished. However, his career has been injury plagued and the Raiders will go to backup Behren Morton should he stumble. Morton is a YOLO passer with arm talent and a general air of chaos. However, the Raiders are confident enough in Morton to have let Donovan Smith walk to Houston.

Unsurprisingly, the Red Raiders embrace idiosyncratic tendencies under defensive coordinator Tim DeRuyter. The veteran DC likes to blur the lines between positions with non-traditional employments of personnel in a 3-3-5 scheme to disguise aggressive blitz packages. To that end, senior interior defensive linemen Jaylon Hutchings and Tony Bradford are constantly slanting, stunting or crossing, even on conventional down and distance. The two squatty tackles both go about 6-0, 300 with high motors and they use their mobility to bounce around and break things that they couldn't otherwise thwart by playing straight up in standard defense.

To add to the chaos, Texas Tech coaches believe that Syracuse transfer 6-5, 235 Steve Linton will be a high level pass rusher from the edge. He didn't do much in New York, but maybe he was paying a high state income tax on his pass rush. They want to employ him on stunts while Bradford and Hutchins career around and catch less athletic offensive linemen wrong-footed. In concert, this approach can be very disruptive. Throw in the two largest press corners in college football mugging receivers outside in seniors Malik Dunlap and Rayshad Williams and you have another layer of difficulty for opposing offenses. Though very big and sticky at the line of scrimmage, Dunlap and Williams can't hold up for long against high quality receivers when the pass rush doesn't get there. However, they can physically dominate pass catchers who lack the skill or speed to threaten them deep. The best – or at least the most important – player on the defense may be safety Dadrion Taylor-Demerson. He's usually left to clean up the mess when Tim DeRuyter's schemes malfunction and as their 3rd leading tackler and interception leader, he does an admirable job. 6-6, 285 Myles Cole looks like departed NFL 1st round draft pick Tyree Wilson but has yet to play like him.

Weaknesses

The Tech offensive line will be poor despite a senior laden group with well over one hundred collective starts. While experience on the offensive line is valuable, talent is as well.

Four of five starters will be playing new positions after a massive offseason shuffle. Last year, the unit gave up 40+ sacks and numerous hits on the quarterback. The accumulation of injuries that Tech quarterbacks suffered wasn't coincidental. Caleb Rogers, despite 29 career starts, will likely continue to struggle as a pass blocker despite flipping from left tackle to right and he is an average run blocker. New left tackle Monroe Mills will flip over from right in hopes that switching two below average tackles will improve them. Tech hopes that their interior will be buoyed by two former Western Kentucky offensive linemen. Guard Cole Spencer is a seventh year senior who missed all of last season with a back and knee injury, but he started 44 games at Western Kentucky before following offensive coordinator Zach Kittley to Lubbock. A career tackle moved to guard, the former 1st Team All Conference CUSA performer should be an asset. He will be joined by fellow Western Kentuckian Rusty Staats, who is a center, not the result of what happens to a calculator left out in a rainstorm. Staats notched 27 starts at WKU and was an above average performer at that level. Lastly, former JUCO walk-on Dennis Milburn will be the right guard after starting 13 games at center last year. In totality, this is not an impressive group but Tech will try to protect them with quick throws and pace.

Playing alongside some of Tech's agents of defensive mayhem are some questionable players at key positions. Linebacker Jesiah Pierre weighs 245 pounds and is very effective at blitzing and not much else as a traditional linebacker (4.5 sacks last year) and his fellow linebacker Jacob Rodriguez is a converted quarterback who was a marginal performer in 2022 playing in spot action. Former Longhorn Tyler Owens is an athletic freak at safety but he's rarely healthy, isn't instinctive and has a grand total of 32 tackles over four years. Texas Tech isn't strong on the second and third levels if you can bypass their interior defensive line and cornerbacks. It's important that offensive play callers not obsess over what Tech is trying to do to them, but rather find, isolate and exploit their defensive weaknesses.

Several Red Raider strengths are potential weaknesses if you solve for them. Prepare your defense for the notion that there are four downs in a possession, not three. Don't concede short gains on 3rd and 4th and short to avoid the threat of big plays. This fundamentally misunderstands what Tech is trying to achieve through volume of attrition. Hurry up offenses that go three and out aren't much of a threat on the sideline. Texas Tech is dangerous only insofar as a defensive coordinator concedes the Raiders' offensive line's ability to protect or fears pressuring their receivers on key downs. Finally, prepare the offense for defensive chaos and Tech's rapid adjustments. Tech's style of play can be gouged for big plays if an offense maintains composure and puts offensive focus on the defenders that Tech is trying to hide.

THE OTHER FOUR

A 14 team Big 12 means that the days of round robins and "true champions" are no longer with us. In fact, some teams lucked out on scheduling (I'm looking at you Oklahoma teams) while Iowa State will play every team in the top half of the league.

These four teams, half of them conference newcomers, don't play Texas, but they will impact the conference race, less likely as legitimate contenders but more as potential upset candidates who could play spoiler to a real aspirant. So here's an overview on the state of the program at UCF, Cincinnati, Oklahoma State and West Virginia.

UCF is probably the most intriguing of the four new league entrants. They have a real coach, a dangerous if limited quarterback and they recruit in the heart of a state that feeds under recruited late bloomers to the NFL with regularity. They're also a prime transfer destination for former ACC and SEC players seeking more playing time or a do over on prior indiscretions. Those Florida State and Auburn second chancers either gloriously implode or ball out to the NFL and that makes the floor and ceiling for the Knights all the more unpredictable and fascinating. UCF has won 59 games over the last six years and they're well positioned to further that success if they can stick to their Florida speed knitting while adding some Texas polish and brawn. Let's not oversell a team that lost to Navy last year, but the theoretical ceiling for UCF is probably much higher than any of the new entrants. At least with regard to upset potential on any given Saturday. Much of that is because of their coach.

Gus Malzahn should change his name to Gus Mayhem. He has a long history of putting together elite game plans for a prestige opponent; a constant irritant for teams with big dreams. Malzahn isn't shy about starting that prestige opponent specific preparation in August or during another opponent's game week. That tendency has bitten Gus in the ass more than once, losing games to lesser opponents that he ignored, but the big upsets he has pulled off tend to overshadow the underachieving gut punches. The bottom line is that Malzahn has a lifetime 94-47 record with an SEC title on his resume and he was the offensive coordinator for a 14-0 Auburn national championship team. If you've coached in the Iron Bowl against a #1 Alabama and called plays in the national title game, a road game in Ames doesn't reduce you to quivering jello. UCF ain't scared to be in the Big 12 and they are confident (or delusional) enough to think that they will be handing out the introductory hard knocks, not taking them.

That confidence comes from their head coach. College football enthusiasts remember the legendary 2013 Kick Six Auburn win over Alabama due to the improbable final play, but forget that game was tied because Auburn's running game dominated Alabama's defense, racking up 5.7 yards per carry and nearly 300 yards rushing. Malzahn would stick it to Saban twice more with strong game plans during his time on the Plains and Alabama week always meant closed media practices and the introduction of novel formations and innovative game plans.

This Malzahn trait is not just Bama specific. Last year, UCF beat top 10 Tulane 38-31 in the regular season with a terrific offensive game plan against the best defense in the league. It's doubtful that UCF can bring sustained play every week due to some fatal flaws on their defense and poor team depth, but their potential to introduce mayhem to the Big 12 race is considerable. Want an easy shorthand for what defines Malzahn's success at UCF? When they rush for 160+ yards, he is 17-2. When they do not? They are 1-7.

Malzahn does not have his best Auburn squads at hand for his first year in the Big 12, but he does have talent at key positions. Starting quarterback John Rhys Plumlee is a strong dual threat in Malzahn's system. Plumlee is a very mediocre passer (he threw for 2,586 yards passing at 7.5 yards per attempt; but sometimes it looks worse than that) and he's a fearless and instinctive runner who notched 862 rushing yards and 11 touchdowns last year despite missing some time with injuries. The former Ole Miss transfer actually had a 1,000 yard rushing season in Oxford as a freshman. Plumlee isn't big and there is a perilous trade off in employing his legs too often. Ultimately if the offense is to level up, Plumlee will have to become a more effective play action passer and distribute the ball better to his receivers and running backs. Malzahn needs to save Plumlee's 15+ carry games for marquee opponents.

The rest of the UCF skill players are talented and fit Malzahn's system well. Wide receiver Javon Baker is a strong-bodied big play stud and is capable of a 1,000+ yard season, Auburn transfer Kobe Hudson is a dangerous deep threat and RJ Harvey and Johnny Richardson are elusive runners that Malzhan will get on the edge with his schematic machinations. The offensive line is questionable and Malzahn will rely on angle advantage blocking, the +1 of Plumlee in the run game and motion smoke and mirrors to help his guys in the trenches. The offensive line will inevitably improve as run blockers over the course of the season, a hallmark of all Malzhan coached offenses. Pass protection will be another matter altogether. Teams that shock UCF's run game and put them into 3rd and predictable will find Plumlee relatively easy to defend if they assign a spy, but good Malzhan offenses have a knack for staying ahead of the chains.

Defensively, UCF has a disruptive front and a productive linebacker in Jason Johnson, but the rest of the back seven is very shaky or simply unknown. The Knights were ineffective defending the pass last year and that probably won't change in 2023 unless transfers and unexpected contributors really come through for them. That does happen in Orlando, so this isn't just blind hope. They will rely heavily on offensive ball control and pressure from the front to shorten games, steal stops and let the offense serve as the 4th quarter closer. The long term prospects for UCF in a post blue blood Big 12 are strong and their 2023 ceiling is probably eight wins if they have good injury luck and a couple of their SEC transfers can get their heads right. The fat part of the bell curve and Plumlee missing a game or three suggests a six or seven win effort and at least one major disruptive upset of a higher ranked team with a classic Malzahn toe-stubbing against a scrub.

What game will Gus Malzahn circle on the 2023 schedule to announce his Big 12 arrival? Well, UCF and Oklahoma both have byes before playing each other in Norman. Interesting.

It's cheaper to keep her may not be the most romantic reason for continuing a marriage, but that phrase has punctuated more than a few deep pulls off of the bottle after a deep sigh. At West Virginia, the bottle holds more resignation than positive spirits as they puzzle through their faded honeymoon with head coach Neal Brown. A marriage whose continuance is now borne more of economic necessity and Brown's lack of suitors than enduring love.

WEST VIRGINIA

2022 RECORD	POINTS SCORED	POINTS ALLOWED
5-7	30.6	32.9
Not Ranked	#51 of 131	#116 of 131

BIG XII CONFERENCE

Neal Brown | 5th season
2022 conference record 3-6

RETURNING STARTERS
OFFENSE - 5 | DEFENSE - 5

In 2023, their best hope is mutual tolerance until the inevitable painful parting. The hard facts of the relationship? If West Virginia parted ways with Brown before 2023, they owed him just over 20 million dollars. After January 1st, 2023? 16.7 million dollars. West Virginia can't afford either price, particularly with the cost of paying the dowry for a new bride. For a university in a state rightfully proud of making do with what you have, the current cost of divorce is too rich. The more interesting question is: how did the price tag get so steep in hardscrabble Appalachia? Why does a sub .500 Neal Brown have the 10th highest buyout in all of college football?

Enter former West Virginia athletic director Shane Lyons, who put on a masterwork class on how to mismanage a prenup. He's not the first athletic director to blink when an agent comes calling for renegotiation when their client achieves some dubious milestone and he won't be the last. Lyons blinked harder than a man in an Arabian sandstorm without his trusty Visine and now he is a deputy athletic director at Alabama, playing Barney Fife to Nick Saban's Andy Griffith.

Don't laugh. Texas has its own history of facial tics confronting fabricating agents spinning tales of NFL or SEC suitors. In 2019, new AD Chris Del Conte needlessly extended Tom Herman after his Sugar Bowl win over Georgia, staving off a whole slew of suitors...that did not exist. However, Texas can erase bad deals and try on new coaches like a wardrobe change. In West Virginia, they can't afford a new outfit when they poop their pants. They get to sit in it for a while.

Neal Brown was signed to a generous six year contract when he took over in 2019, but after a 11-11 start in his first two years, his AD Lyons found himself positively giddy with the trajectory of the program – a Liberty Bowl win over Army during a COVID year! – and imagining SEC poachers that did not exist (seeded by Brown's agent) luring away his valuable .500 prize, Lyons extended Brown's six year contract another two years before Brown had even completed Year 3; agreeing to a 100% buyout of Brown's contract if he was let go before 2025, with an 85% payout up to 2026. That's wholly irresponsible in every fiduciary sense and in college athletics, pretty common. Spending other people's money is awesome!

Lyons also layered in significant buy out penalties should another program suitor come calling, trapping Brown and WVU in a mutual death embrace. Athletic directors who don't understand how markets work think buyouts protect them, but buyouts marry programs to problem children who could otherwise seek a mutually beneficial exit. The rare superstar that it supposedly protects from covetous big programs is denied their professional fulfillment. Making your most important athletic revenue generator angry and resentful to be in a job that requires wholehearted commitment and 70 hour weeks is not a great plan. So as the shine has come off of Brown's moon, West Virginia has little hope for a mutual parting of ways as it had with preceding head coach Dana Holgorsen, a mutual good riddance enabled by Holgo's very friendly one million dollar buyout.

Entering his 5th year in Morgantown, Brown boasts a 22-25 overall record, a single winning season (6-4 in 2020) and, most tellingly, a 14-21 Big 12 record. That 40% winning percentage in Big 12 play particularly galls Mountaineer fans and 2022's 3-6 (5-7 overall) record suggests that Brown and West Virginia find themselves back where they started in 2019, when the enthusiastic program builder from Troy (where he boasted a 35-16 history) promised a building process he dubbed The Climb. In the five years prior to Brown's hire, West Virginia was 27-18 in conference play and boasted five consecutive winning seasons. Brown's tenure has been The Descent.

It turns out that the real Klieman was being done at Kansas State. You paid for the preview, but the Dad jokes are free.

The problem for West Virginia is that while Brown can't succeed, he won't just egregiously fail. West Virginia generally plays very hard, albeit with decreasing talent each year. Brown's teams keep losing the portal math equation and that arithmetic is cruel. However, Mountaineer fans admire pluck and resilience, even in a losing effort, and Brown keeps signing nearly respectable recruiting classes. This is the slim peddling of hope, deeply seductive to their fanbase's underdog psychology. Even as West Virginia faded last year, they won 2 of their last 3, upsetting Oklahoma in Morgantown and polishing off a death spiraling Oklahoma State in Stillwater. They played Backyard Brawl rival Pitt tough in the opener, beat Baylor after Blake Shapen went down and pummeled Virginia Tech on the road. Virginia Tech is a horrific football team, but there's still name brand recognition and the average fan thinks that they still have Michael Vick. A proper failing program would full on quit and force the administration's hand through repeated humiliations, but Brown keeps stringing along his fanbase on bare threads of thin hope.

The portal problems still persist. Pretty much the entire Mountaineer wide receiver corps – who all had the option to return in 2023 and would have been one of the better units in the league – said sayonara. West Virginia also loses their best three defenders on an already poor defense and all of their defensive front to the NFL Draft or transfer (Taijh Alston will start at Colorado, Jordan Jefferson to LSU). Their prospects for 2023 are Appalachian February bleak and if their on-field scrappiness relents even a little, full on disaster is guaranteed. In today's college football landscape, any program without a natural recruiting base that can't win in the portal and retain 5th and 6th year homegrown players has zero chance of success. That's West Virginia.

The Big 12 did take pity on Neal Brown and scheduled West Virginia to play all four new conference additions. Going 3-1 or 2-2 against that mix would be helpful, but prior athletic directors left them the non-conference scheduling gifts of a road opener at Penn State and their continued series with Pittsburgh. Well, at least there's always Duquesne. The offense promises to be bad to below average and anyone who can stop a decent running game premised on running back CJ Donaldson's rumbles and quarterback Garrett Greene's scrambling improvisation will have their way with them.

Last year, West Virginia prayed and then punted on a coaching change under new AD Wren Baker. Outside of a miracle revival, the decision is now not if but when they decide to swallow the buyout and move on from Neal Brown. The Mountaineers are a cautionary tale and should be a required case study for every college athletic director, particularly those who manage programs with little margin for error and cannot rescue bad decision making with blank checks. Fortunately for coaches and agents, no one has much time for parables or case studies and the cycle of overly enthusiastic athletic directors bidding against themselves will continue unabated.

CINCINNATI BEARCATS

2022 RECORD	POINTS SCORED	POINTS ALLOWED
9-4	29.2	20.6
Not Ranked	#59 of 131	#20 of 131

BIG XII CONFERENCE
Scott Satterfield | 1st season
2022 conference record 6-2

RETURNING STARTERS
OFFENSE - 2 | DEFENSE - 6

Bearcat coaching hires over the last two decades have been impressive. Men like Mark Dantonio, Butch Jones, Brian Kelly, Tommy Tuberville and Luke Fickell grew the program from an irrelevant afterthought to a regional powerhouse that dominated the American Athletic Conference, struck fear in non-conference Power 5 opponents and even earned them an improbable college football playoff appearance. Before you think that last achievement was a pure fluke, that Bearcat playoff team had 9 players taken in the 2022 NFL draft. Only Georgia and LSU had more that year. That's one hell of a developmental program given average recruiting classes ranked in the 40s and 50s. The guy who did that now coaches at Wisconsin.

Cincinnati has long been a stepping stone school, elevating its former coaches to jobs like Michigan State, Tennessee, Notre Dame and Wisconsin, but nearly always reloading with an inspired hire. After losing head coach Luke Fickell to Wisconsin (who should share some notes on career timing with Matt Campbell) Cincinnati starts over with a new head man: former Louisville head coach Scott Satterfield.

When you add Satterfield to the list of coaches that preceded him, one of these things is not quite like the others. Satterfield coached Louisville for four years, compiling a 25-24 record (and a 15-18 ACC conference mark). The native North Carolinian also has no ties to Ohio, the Midwest or Texas. The lateral move felt more like a coach staying ahead of the posse, leaving Louisville on his own terms rather than the terms that may be later imposed on him. Terms like: "Please put your things in this cardboard box while security walks you out, Coach Satterfield."

If he bears resemblance to any of his Bearcat coaching predecessors, it's Tommy Tuberville, who fled an unsuccessful Texas Tech experiment for Cincy, eager to get away from an increasingly untenable situation in Lubbock. It's probably not a coincidence that Tuberville's reign in Cincinnati was the least impressive of the last twenty years. He was 4-8 in his final season. No one is confusing hiring Scott Satterfield with Brian Kelly. He's not half the coach that Kelly is and he doesn't turn deep shades of pink whenever his offense gets an illegal motion penalty.

Coaching questions aside, do the Bearcats have any ballers?

A few. Not as many as they need. The Bearcats spent the offseason bleeding out from the portal and they brought back only two offensive starters. Quarterback also takes on a new look after solid starter Ben Bryant transferred to Northwestern in May, reluctant to share snaps with former Arizona State and Florida starter Emory Jones. Jones is a 6th year dual threat with 20 collegiate starts under his belt, but he lost his job at each of his two prior stops. The offensive line is unready for prime time and will break in four new starters that transferred in from schools like Penn and Southeast Missouri State, respectively. They must replace their entire wide receiver corps (their top six pass catchers are gone, two to the NFL) and while they did bring in some portal talent to stem the blood loss, the whole offensive product looks slapdash and incoherent. This will be one of the worst offenses in the Big 12 even if their new dual threat passer puts the entire unit on his back every Saturday.

The defense looks reasonably talented overall with a particularly strong defensive front.. Defensive tackles Dontay Corleone (PFF's highest ranked defender in the country, 3rd team All-American) and Jowon Briggs (1st team All-AAC) are very high level players with NFL futures and they bring in talented edge candidates from Utah State and Louisville to solidify the front as one of the league's best. This will be a physical and explosive pass rushing group and that does offer them some interesting potential matched up against subpar offensive lines. The secondary could be decent, their upside resting on transfer corners from Arizona State and Florida. The Bearcats will create a lot of tackles for loss and should be near the league's leaders in sacks, but if you can block them up, offensive inadequacy, a questionable secondary, and their lack of depth will cost them. Expect the Cincy coaching staff to emphasize the running game, lean on their defensive front and pray that the opponent self-destructs.

They do get a massive scheduling break: no Texas, Texas Tech, Kansas State or TCU. That's great luck and it should cushion the adjustment as they take on the league's dregs.

Non-conference contests against Miami of Ohio and Eastern Kentucky will also inflate the win total of what should be a firmly below average football team. The Bearcats have had a terrific two decade run of blue skies and green fields, but their present and future are cloudy in a league where they have no natural recruiting base and a head coach who is there more out of necessity than desire.

OKLAHOMA STATE COWBOYS

2022 RECORD	POINTS SCORED	POINTS ALLOWED
7-6	30.6	28.9
Not Ranked	#49 of 131	#89 of 131

BIG XII CONFERENCE
Mike Gundy | 19th season
2022 conference record 4-5

RETURNING STARTERS
OFFENSE - 7 | DEFENSE - 2

The Cowboys had a disappointing end to their 2022 season, losing 5 of their last 6 games after upsetting Texas in Stillwater. Those losses included blow outs by Kansas and Kansas State, a firm defeat by struggling rival Oklahoma and they even bowed to a bad West Virginia. Oklahoma State certainly brought their best against Texas, but an exceedingly poor Longhorn second half by Texas and a rather unprecedented 14-0 pro Cowboy penalty deficit abetted a 41-34 upset. Oklahoma State would limp to a 7-6 record overall, including an unwatchable bowl performance. Still, that was Mike Gundy's 17th consecutive winning season at Oklahoma State, moving him to a 156-75 career mark. That's an impressive achievement and discounting one of the best and most underappreciated coaches in college football is foolhardy, but the cracks in the program are too many to be papered over by "Don't ever bet against Mike Gundy!" platitudes. It's a particularly interesting platitude because it's being uttered by really smart people relying on their intensive study of Gundy's history and his ability to find unconventional solutions and also some really dumb people reciting something that they read in Athlon.

Oklahoma State returns only two defensive starters and will break in a new defensive coordinator, Bryan Nardo from Gannon University. One nice thing about Gundy hires is that you learn about obscure colleges that you never knew existed. Also nice? – Gundy perpetually reminds us that there are potentially good coaches at every level of football. Gundy's ability to find quality at Dollar General while everyone is canvassing Whole Foods is laudable and proof that football coaching talent is not found in a perfect bell curve distribution at the best jobs. That written, a third new defensive system in the last three years combined with barely mediocre overall talent does not bode well for hopes of a stifling Cowboy defense. A functional defense is the 2023 goal, even if the Cowboys do have some bright spots.

The good news is that edge/linebacker Collin Oliver and safety Kendal Daniels are top notch talent to build an identity around and the spring raves around Utah Tech transfer nose tackle Justin Kirkland (all 6-4, 350 of him) are considerable. The bad news is that the other positions (and the depth behind them) are a clear step down from the types of high level defensive personnel that they had in Stillwater as recently as 2021. An analyst can squint and see a path to decent defense, but it requires a lot of optimism, deep faith in player development and a thick pair of beer goggles.

In past defensive transition years Gundy typically just outscored everyone and had a successful year anyway, but there are major questions on offense as well. Former Texas Tech starter turned Michigan 3rd stringer Alan Bowman will start at quarterback after four year Cowboy starter Spencer Sanders transferred to Ole Miss. Bowman's slow feet can't extend plays as well as he has extended his college eligibility, but Gundy is favorably disposed to Bowman's skill set after he lit up the Cowboys for 781 yards and 5 touchdowns in his two starts against them while he was in Lubbock. Gundy sees things in certain players that other coaches don't perceive and Bowman brings an element to the offense that Gundy wants to reintroduce: timing and rhythm.

Sanders preferred to ad lib, creating huge plays for both Oklahoma State and the opponent, but he also removed much of the precision that the offense enjoyed with quarterbacks like Brandon Weeden and Mason Rudolph. Bowman won't have anything like the wide receivers those men did, but it is a decent bet in any given year that the Cowboys will always find at least adequate pass catchers. They return very solid slot Brennan Presley (67 catches, 813 yards) and add veteran wideout De'Zhaun Stribling from Washington State (a combined 95 catches and 10 touchdowns over two years). A lack of receiver depth on the heels of multiple transfers exiting also suggests that running backs Ollie Gordon, Elijah Collins and Jaden Nixon will get plenty of work running the ball.

Who will block for this new look offense? The Cowboys have not had a good offensive line for some time and 2023 will be no different. Gundy will do his best to disguise those deficiencies, but any defense that can stop the run honestly and play tight coverage to disrupt

Bowman's rhythm and timing passing game will likely destroy them. The good news for Oklahoma State is that destroyers are in short supply on their schedule. Big 12 headquarters subscribes to the notion that Cowboys ride for free and that's reflected in a schedule absent Texas, Texas Tech, TCU and Baylor. So Oklahoma State avoids an 0-4 or 1-3 run of opponent results and trades them out with the likes of Houston, West Virginia, Cincy, Iowa State and BYU. That's a remarkable gift, one Gundy values even more than an industrial sized bottle of Aqua Net. A feeble conference slate might create a mirage record that may allow Gundy to narrowly continue his winning ways, suggesting a still blooming oasis in Stillwater, but closer examination will reveal dry holes, tumbleweeds and dust.

2023 LONGHORN FOOTBALL SCHEDULE

WEEK 1	SEPTEMBER 2	AUSTIN, TX
WEEK 2	SEPTEMBER 9	TUSCALOOSA, AL
WEEK 3	SEPTEMBER 16	AUSTIN, TX
WEEK 4	SEPTEMBER 23	WACO, TX
WEEK 5	SEPTEMBER 30	AUSTIN, TX
WEEK 6	OCTOBER 7	DALLAS, TX
WEEK 7	OCTOBER 21	HOUSTON, TX
WEEK 8	OCTOBER 28	AUSTIN, TX
WEEK 9	NOVEMBER 4	AUSTIN, TX
WEEK 10	NOVEMBER 11	FORT WORTH, TX
WEEK 11	NOVEMBER 18	AMES, IA
WEEK 12	NOVEMBER 24	AUSTIN, TX
BIG XII CHAMPIONSHIP	DECEMBER 2	DALLAS, TX

The Longhorns face a challenging, but workable schedule. Six home games and the Horns only leave the state of Texas twice.

Rice and Wyoming are home game wins bracketing a trip to Bama.

Road games at Houston and at Iowa State may offer rabid environments but team quality, not environment, tends to determine outcomes. If Iowa State hopes to foist an upset, a Jon Heacock game plan will be at the center of it.

Texas gets Kansas in DKR with Longhorn advantages on both lines of scrimmage. BYU has to travel to Texas and Taysom Hill has no remaining eligibility.

TCU in mid-November in Fort Worth could be a team that has found its legs after an easy opening schedule, but also a team about to catch their third consecutive loss after preceding road trips to Kansas State and Texas Tech.

Is Baylor clearly better than some of the teams listed before them? Probably not. But they are the road conference opener and last year Texas was caught wrong-footed in the same scenario in Lubbock. Baylor plays Long Island the week prior. I wonder if they will be working on Texas stuff that week? Win that game in Waco or face very uncomfortable questions about staff and team preparation.

Kansas State comes to DKR. Styles make fights and the Wildcat defenses don't match up well to Texas.

Texas Tech will face a fired up Texas and a raucous crowd. In truth, you could have them switch spots with Oklahoma, but home field can't be discounted.

The Red River Shootout is defined by its upsets. Oklahoma isn't a better team than KSU or Texas Tech but a weak Sooner schedule means that a win over Texas puts them in the driver's seat for the Big 12 title game. While Texas works on Bama in August, Oklahoma will be working on Texas. Count on that.

Alabama has chinks in their armor, but a night game in Tuscaloosa is not for the faint of heart. The last team to win there was 2019 national champion LSU in a 46-41 shootout. Since 2008, Alabama is 84-5 at home. Is that good?

BIG XII CONFERENCE PREDICTIONS

Team	Wins	Losses
Texas	8	1
Texas Tech	6	3
Kansas State	6	3
Oklahoma	6	3
TCU	5	4
Kansas	5	4
UCF	5	4
Baylor	5	4
Oklahoma State	4	5
Iowa State	3	6
BYU	3	6
Houston	3	6
West Virginia	2	7
Cincinnati	2	7

TEXAS LONGHORNS DRAFTED

Year	Picks
2013	🐂 🐂 🐂
2014	
2015	🐂 🐂 🐂 🐂 🐂
2016	🐂
2017	🐂
2018	🐂 🐂 🐂 🐂
2019	🐂 🐂
2020	🐂 🐂 🐂 🐂
2021	🐂 🐂 🐂 🐂 🐂
2022	
2023	🐂 🐂 🐂 🐂 🐂

Texas had five players drafted in the 2023 NFL Draft Class, matching a high water mark achieved twice previously in the last decade. Over the last ten years, Texas has averaged three NFL draft picks per year, but has also been skunked twice, most recently in 2022. Standout running back Bijan Robinson went 8th overall to the Falcons. DeMarvion Overshown was taken in the 3rd round by the Dallas Cowboys. Roschon Johnson went to Chicago in the 4th, Keondre Coburn was selected in the 6th round to Kansas City and Moro Ojomo went to the Eagles in the 7th round. This is evidence that Texas is doing a better job developing talent. Further evidence? The 2024 Longhorn draft class could realistically feature eight draft picks.

2023 Recruiting Class

Special Guest Contributor Eric Nahlin, Managing Editor at Inside Texas

By now you've read a lot of burnt orange tinted words from the typically measured Paul Wadlington. Things will only get rosier from here as we discuss what I believe will be the best recruiting class from the Mack Brown era forward.

If you think that's a bold statement keep in mind I'm cheating. Hindsight is 20/20, but insight can be as well and we have the insight of how many of these young men have already transitioned from highly touted recruit to college football player. That transition period has claimed many blue-chip recruits -- I can see right now you're naming them in your head. But thanks to focused mental evaluation by the Texas staff, on top of obvious talent, that won't be the narrative when all is told with this class. Indeed, many of the most talented players in the 2023 class are also the most likely to succeed thanks to their work ethic.

That's the foundation of my optimism. The Arch Mannings, Malik Muhammads, Johntay Cooks, Anthony Hills, CJ Baxters, et al, are not just athletically predestined for success, they're hardwired to maximize.

In keeping with the spirit of Thinking Texas Football, we won't just detail the 2023 class as recruits, we'll offer you the most current inside information from their first days, weeks, and months as Texas Longhorns.

Arch Manning, QB, On3 Industry Ranking 99.53, Natl. 1, 5-star

For a couple of reasons, forget the last name. He's every bit the recruit you'd expect with that ranking regardless of his name. Second, he's different from the common familiarity of what constitutes a Manning. If you're older, he has some Archie Manning athletic qualities, like his father Cooper who played wide receiver. That doesn't mean he's a dual threat, but he's also not going to be targeted by a flock of geese. Forget what the talking heads said about his spring game. That was a loaded test for the former five-star and he didn't perform nearly as poorly as your local expert would have you believe. Manning is already a very popular player in the locker room and helping to push competition in the quarterback room.

Anthony Hill, LB, On3 IR 97.87, Natl. 16, 5-star

A cheat code for identifying good linebackers is imagining them as running backs. With Anthony Hill, we didn't have to imagine. At Denton Guyer he displayed all the explosive

traits and movement skills that will follow him at linebacker as a running back. In his short time on campus, the early enrollee has demonstrated elite pass rushing traits. Because off-ball linebacker typically requires an adjustment period, expect the staff to carve out a role for him as a 'point and shoot' pass rusher in his first season. They will also give him every chance to win the Will linebacker position, but pass rush is the initial priority. The staff flipped Hill from Texas A&M in the middle of the Aggies' disastrous season.

CJ Baxter, RB, On3 IR 97.26, Natl. 30, 5-star

You have Texas running backs coach Tashard Choice to thank for making this steal from Florida look routine. Bijan Robinson's success didn't hurt either. Baxter has an elite blend of size, speed, and running back nuance to his game. Given the opportunity available this season, expect him to be part of a one-two punch with Jonathon Brooks. He had a strong Spring and received high marks for the way he approaches the game. He's the mirror

opposite of Hill — equal parts athletic gifts, size, and want-to, just on the offensive side of the ball rather than defensive.

Johntay Cook, WR, On3 IR 97.23, Natl. 31, 5-star

Cook isn't one of the five fastest at his position but he's one of the quickest and most technically savvy on top of not being slow. Many will recall the long touchdown he had in

the Spring game, but that was a pretty routine play for him. Cook has the swagger you want at the position backed up by his tireless effort. As he physically matures, he's going to be able to win before and after the catch, on the ground and in the air. Cook is going to play a lot this year but he has experienced ballers ahead of him at outside receiver. Year 2 will likely be his breakout year.

Malik Muhammad, CB, On3 IR 96.22, Natl. 49, 4-star

As a player he's the mirror opposite of Cook. As a person, he comes from a family of business-minded entrepreneurs. He attacks football like it's a business — from his diet, to

technique, and to understanding the game from a coach's point of view. He's put himself on the fast track to success and could even start this season despite being in a loaded, experienced room.

Derek Williams, S, On3 IR 95.52, Natl. 62, 4-star

Nicknamed The Raptor because of his athletic, on-field disposition, but away from the field he's a quiet, focused athlete. Unlike the five signees listed before him, Williams wasn't an early enrollee. That written, he's already making up for lost time. Safety, like linebacker and quarterback, is not an easy position to make an early impact, but expect big things in Year

2 for Williams. With the additions of Manning and Williams, Texas stole the best player on each side of the ball from Louisiana.

Ryan Niblett, WR, On3 IR 95.43, Natl. 66, 4-star

Niblett doesn't have Cook's technical refinement at the position but he's a rocket on the field with 10.4 sprinter's speed and 23' 8.5" long jump explosiveness. If you want a good sign of team culture, Niblett didn't enroll early but the second he arrived on campus Johntay Cook and DeAndre Moore took him under their wing to get him caught up on the playbook and route running. In his one month on campus, Niblett has shown improved technique at the position after playing 'athlete' in high school.

Jelani McDonald, ATH, On3 IR 95.03, Natl. 74, 4-star

I'm always leery of 'athletes' because that's not an actual position. As an evaluator you have to envision the player in a specific fit, and that fit at Texas will be linebacker despite him starting his career at Star (nickel). It's always important to know how a player is hardwired when he's going to spin towards a more physical position. In that regard, McDonald fields high marks for his football disposition. That's no surprise, his father played linebacker at TCU. Don't expect much this year but long-term he profiles to either Will or Mike linebacker thanks to his overall ability, athleticism, and football character.

Colton Vasek, EDGE, On3 IR 94.31, Natl. 96, 4-star

Vasek's father Brian played the same position at Texas and also coached his son at Austin Westlake. So when I say Vasek is technically advanced, that's not a stereotypical way of saying he's white. He's much more than technically advanced, though. He's similar to Baxter and Hill in that he is already physically mature but nowhere close to what he'll be in a couple of years. He profiles for the same position as Barryn Sorrell and I believe there are similarities in their play-style and approach to the game. I don't know if Vasek will be flashy in his early years, but he'll become an effective player who plays the run and pass equally well. There's a decent chance he'll blossom into a star. Given need he could see playing time this season. The staff flipped Vasek from OU in the midst of the Sooners' disappointing season.

DeAndre Moore, WR, On3 IR 93.90, Natl. 110, 4-star

Moore was one of the most frequently mentioned early enrollees throughout Spring ball. The repeating theme with him was speed, speed, speed. In fourth place was his readiness to play early. You know Steve Sarkisian has a soft spot for recruits from Southern California but there's no bias in this evaluation. Like Cook, Moore should play a fair amount this year. Expect him to be Jordan Whittington's primary backup if Sark is going like for like with a slot receiver but Moore could also play outside.

Tausili Akana, EDGE, On3 IR 93.50, Natl. 131, 4-star

It was only a matter of time before defensive coordinator Pete Kwiatkowski and linebackers coach Jeff Choate established a pipeline into Polynesian football. With the signing of Akana and linebacker Liona Lefau, both coaches announced Texas as a permanent fixture within that tight-knit community. Akana will require some time to physically mature but the staff targeted him with one purpose in mind — getting after the passer.

Derion Gullette, LB, On3 IR 93.34, Natl. 140, 4-star

The projection on Gullette is in limbo due to a knee injury suffered last Summer, but before that he was one of the most explosive athletes in the country and not just for someone with a linebacker body type. At this point, his body type is actually more in line with EDGE than linebacker, so you're getting an idea of how uncommon Gullette is. He'll be a full participant for Fall camp but as an off-ball linebacker he'll need to incubate before he's ready. Long term it's easy to see him become a hyper-athletic pass rusher.

Jaydon Chatman, OL, On3 IR 91.87, Natl. 214, 4-star

On3 lists Chatman as an interior o-lineman but he's more athletic than the typical guard and spent his time at right tackle during the Spring. It's too early to have expectations beyond what we knew of him as a recruit, but he has turned heads in his short time on campus, including for his work in the weight room.

Sydir Mitchell, DL, On3 IR 91.59, Natl. 226, 4-star

This is one of the poorest rankings you'll find. While some concern is understandable, Mitchell is a giant athlete who is young for his grade. There are only 2-3 guys like him in a given year. Texas beat Georgia for him, what else do you need to know? He's made good strides on acclimating to college and reshaping his body. He'll play some this season but expect a much larger timeshare in Texas' first season in the SEC. He is one of the most important signees in the entire class when you factor in roster needs.

Warren Roberson, S, On3 IR 90.89, Natl. 272, 4-star

On3 was the outlier in its high ranking for the twitched up athlete. Roberson is very similar to Jordan Whittington, only he prefers safety rather than wide receiver. He is already one of the best athletes on the team but he'll require some time before he's ready to play. Just a very strong blend of athleticism, ball-hawking ability, and defensive mindset.

S'Maje Burrell, LB, On3 IR 90.17, Natl. 316, 4-star

When you look at Burrell you initially see a barrel-chested throwback at the position, but then he posts footage demonstrating his effortless ability to back flip and you remember he's a legit athlete. Unlike a few others at his position he didn't enroll early. That hurts his chances for an immediate impact but the depth chart thins out considerably after this year and you can expect him to play in 2024.

Trevor Goosby, OT, On3 IR 89.16, Natl. 415, 3-star

Goosby represents a bit of a departure from Kyle Flood's preferred approach of taking giant athletes and slimming them down. Goosby is not small at 6-foot-6, but at 275 he'll need to beef up before he's ready. He's shown great work ethic in the gym. That's a great sign, because we already know he's a tremendous athlete given his ability in basketball and throwing the shot. Goosby placed fifth in the Class 5A state track and field meet with a throw of 56' 5.25". That coordination, bend, and explosiveness is not common in an offensive tackle. Kelvin Banks having two years remaining is a gift to Goosby and his developmental timeline.

Liona Lefau, LB, On3 IR 89.03, Natl. 425, 3-star

If there's one player flying under the radar it's the Hawaiian Lefau. To get an idea of his talent level the staff prioritized him every bit as much as Anthony Hill. Once Lefau was committed he actually helped recruit Hill. The duo should pair perfectly as a do-it-all Mike and Will linebacker combo. Lefau will gain valuable experience this year before replacing Jaylan Ford in 2024. He is uncommon in his comfort playing the pass while also fulfilling traditional linebacker run-plugging duties.

Tre Wisner, RB, On3 IR 89.00, Natl. 438, 3-star

Wisner's running style is best described as slashing. He gets small through the hole before accelerating into the second level. There's a bit of a logjam at running back, but don't be surprised if the staff eventually looks at him as a slot receiver. He reminded everyone of his athletic ability in DeSoto's state championship victory as he made big play after big play from the inside receiver position. That said, he's impressed with his work ethic at running back in his short time on campus.

Billy Walton, EDGE, On3 IR 88.55, Natl. 488, 3-star

Another state champion, Walton starred at Dallas South Oak Cliff with his cousin Malik Muhammad. While Muhammad garnered much of the recruiting press, the staff was all in on the one-time Oklahoma State commit. Walton didn't arrive in Austin until late May, but he has already demonstrated quality pass rushing skill. While he doesn't have a big frame, there's no concern whether he'll eventually carry the needed 245 pounds or so for the position.

Payton Kirkland, OT, On3 IR 88.28, Natl. 532, 3-star

Sydir Mitchell, Liona Lefau, and Payton Kirkland are the three biggest ranking misses in the class. Kirkland is a massive offensive tackle with surprising agility and bend. If he starts to throw his weight around and embrace the physical side of the sport there's nothing keeping him from an NFL career. He's a candidate to see time at guard to earn experience before playing tackle as need arises.

Connor Stroh, OL, On3 IR 88.25, Natl. 547, 3-star

He looks and lifts like a World's Strongest Man competitor. Evaluation and projection have to account for trend lines and Stroh is on a good one. He was injured for most of his sophomore year which had him flying under the radar. He also carried far too much weight. Since then he has leaned up while increasing strength. He is already one of the strongest players in the program, but his career will be defined by how quickly he can move his feet. If he increases his quickness he becomes a quality starter at guard.

Spencer Shannon, TE, On3 IR 87.30, Natl. 699, 3-star

Ultimately football is about getting players in the right fit. Along those lines, if you rank Shannon as an in-line blocking tight end he's elite. That's not the sexiest position and the reason why he's ranked where he is, but when he's eventually neutralizing a defensive end and allowing Sark to take advantage of numbers he's going to become a very big, if unheralded, part of the offense. He's a bigger Geoff Swaim and that's quite the compliment.

Andre Cojoe, OL, On3 IR 87.05, Natl. 736, 3-star

If you've ever wondered why offensive line rankings can be so hit or miss it's because of the gestation period where careers are made or lost. Players with good baseline ability who stay the developmental course often overshoot their original projection. Texas' starting right tackle Christian Jones is a very good example of this. Cojoe didn't turn 17-years old until a week after he arrived on campus in January. While his floor as a player is low, his ceiling is very high if he embraces the grind. He's currently being groomed at tackle but he could become an excellent guard.

Will Randle, TE, On3 IR 86.33, Natl. 855, 3-star

The football ecosystem is fixated on the Travis Kelce, Brock Bowers freaks of nature but there's still a place for the skilled, intelligent, coordinated, and tough tight ends of the world. Randle has a chance to become a multi-purpose tight end who surprises defenses with his receiving ability. He is coming off a knee injury his senior season but rehab has gone very well. Don't expect much this season but he and Shannon could become a quietly good and complementary tandem in the years ahead.

**

Thanks for reading the 11th annual Burnt Orange Bible. Please share it with your tribe and write a 5 star review on Amazon. Your readership is vital in allowing us to create a great product and it can't continue without your support on social media and through your Texas Exes groups. Thanks for Thinking Texas Football with us and Hook 'em!

About the Authors/Creators

Paul Wadlington is a Texas graduate, author, podcaster, partner in a financial business, commercial real estate investor and inveterate entrepreneur currently living in Colorado Springs, Colorado. You'll find Paul writing at Inside Texas and on the Everyone Gets A Trophy podcast. Feel free to reach out at trophymailbag@gmail.com

Will Gallagher is a talented professional photographer, Austin native and Texas graduate whose work can be found at http://gallagherstudios.com. He has been with Inside Texas since 2003. Will provided the incredible photos that enrich this preview.

Eric Nahlin is a recruiting industry expert, Longhorn insider, and the managing partner at Inside Texas. He lives in Houston...if you define Houston by the endless suburbs and small towns that border the actual city, which is how everyone defines it.